THE BHADRAMĀYĀKĀRAVYĀKARAṆA

THE BHADRAMĀYĀKĀRAVYĀKARAṆA

INTRODUCTION, TIBETAN TEXT, TRANSLATION AND NOTES

KONSTANTY RÉGAMEY

Foreword by
JACQUES MAY

MOTILAL BANARSIDASS PUBLISHERS
PVT. LTD. • DELHI

First Published: Warsaw, 1938
First Indian Edition: Delhi, 1990

ISBN: 81-208-0761-8

Also available at:
MOTILAL BANARSIDASS
41 U.A., Bungalow Road, Jawahar Nagar, Delhi 110 007
120 Royapettah High Road, Mylapore, Madras 600 004
24 Race Course Road, Bangalore 560 001
Ashok Rajpath, Patna 800 004
Chowk, Varanasi 221 001

PRINTED IN INDIA
BY JAINENDRA PRAKASH JAIN AT SHRI JAINENDRA PRESS, A-45 NARAINA INDUSTRIAL AREA, PHASE I, NEW DELHI 110 028 AND PUBLISHED BY NARENDRA PRAKASH JAIN FOR MOTILAL BANARSIDASS PUBLISHERS PVT. LTD., BUNGALOW ROAD, JAWAHAR NAGAR, DELHI 110 007.

FOREWORD

Konstanty Régamey (1907-1982) began his scientific career by publishing two works in Warsaw in the same year, 1938. These were the *Three Chapters of the Samādhirājasūtra* and the *Bhadra-māyākāra-vyākaraṇa*, both of which have now been reprinted by Motilal Banarsidass to the great satisfaction of specialists in Indian and Buddhist studies.

The *Bhadra-māyākāra-vyākaraṇa*, "The Prophecy of the Magician Bhadra", is part of the great collection entitled *Ratnakūṭa*, "Multitude of Jewels", a collection much revered in the Buddhist Mahāyāna traditions of Tibet and China. While it is not one of the more important of the 49 *sūtras* included in the *Ratnakūṭa*, it is, in itself, an apologue full of charm and irony which has its value in its literary qualities, merits which are, as Régamey himself mentioned, rare in this type of literature.

Régamey's plan was that the *Bhadra-māyākāra-vyākaraṇa* should inaugurate a series entitled, "Minor Ratnakūṭa Sūtras". The series got no further than its first volume. The project had a resurgence in the form of an edition and translation of the *Upāli-paripṛcchā* published in 1973 by Pierre Python, a student of Konstanty Régamey at the University of Fribourg in Switzerland. It was in this same university that Régamey consecrated a seminar to reading another "minor Ratnakūṭa Sūtra", the *Dṛḍhādhyāśaya-saṃcodana-sūtra*; but, to our knowledge, nothing was ever published.[1]

The stock of the 1938 edition of the *Bhadra-māyākāra-vyākaraṇa* perished in the destruction of Warsaw during the Second World War, making Régamey's work one of extreme scarcity. The present reprint by Motilal Banarsidass is, therefore, all the more welcome indeed.*

JACQUES MAY

---

1 Note that an English translation of the *Bhadra-māyākāra-vyākaraṇa*, made on the basis of the Chinese version, is to be found in: *A Treasury of Mahāyāna Sūtras*. Selections from the Mahāratnakūṭa Sūtra . . . Garma C.C. Chang, General Editor, University Park and London, Pennsylvania University Press, 1983.

* My thanks to Dr. Tom Tillemans for kindly having rendered my text into English.

CONTENTS

Introduction

1. The so called *Ratnakūṭa* collection of the Mahāyāna sūtras constitutes a comparatively modern classification which was unknown to Indian authorities like Sthiramati or Śāntideva[1], and was not mentioned in China before the beginning of the VIIIth century. It was adopted later on by the editors of the Tibetan Kanjur. But it is precisely the late date of the compilation of the *Ratnakūṭa* which leads to the conclusion that this series is a collection of the most important and renowned texts which really deserved the name of »Accumulation of Jewels« and had been assembled in one group for practical purposes.

In fact, among the sūtras belonging to this section of the Tripiṭaka, we find very ancient works such as the *Kāśyapaparivarta;* famous philosophical texts like *Pitāputrasamāgama*, *Śrīmālādevīsiṃhanādasūtra*, *Ugradattaparipṛcchā*, or the very important treatise of the Mahāyānistic *vinaya* the *Upāliparipṛcchā*. All those texts are very often quoted in later compendiums like the *Śikṣāsamuccaya*, *Bodhicaryāvatāra*, *Mādhyamikavṛtti*, etc.

Yet, in spite of its importance, the *Ratnakūṭa* has been very little investigated as yet. From the 49 texts classified under this collective title in the Chinese Tripiṭaka and in the Kanjur, only four are preserved in the original idiom and edited: *Sukhāvatīvyūha*[2], *Rāṣṭrapālaparipṛcchā*[3], *Kāśyapaparivartta*[4] and *Saptaśatikāprajñā-*

---

[1] Cf. Baron A. von Staël-Holstein, *The Kāśyapaparivarta*, Shanghai 1926.

[2] Ed. by Max Müller, Anecdota Oxoniensia, Aryan Series, vol. I, Part II, Oxford 1883.

[3] Ed. by L. Finot, Bibliotheca Buddhica nº II, St. Petersbourg 1901.

[4] Cf. note 1.

pāramitā[5]. Fragments of the *Ratnarāśisūtra*[6] have been edited by F. W. Thomas[7], a great part of the *Upāliparipṛcchā* has been published by Nalinaksha Dutt[8]. As for the rest, we have only quotations in later literature and the Chinese translations contained in the Taishō edition.

Since there remain very few chances to discover the Indian originals of the other texts of *Ratnakūṭa*, it seems that at least the most important works of this series should be rendered accessible, and that an edition of the sources which are at our disposal is urgently required.

The study of the *Ratnakūṭa* might begin with the editions of shorter texts which, though no less important, can be sooner worked out. The present writer intends to bring out an edition of a series of »*Minor Ratnakūṭa Sūtras*« and the first of those texts is the *Bhadramāyākāravyākaraṇa* (n° 21 of the *Ratnakūṭa*).

My attention was attracted to this short sūtra by the work of Ernst Leumann, *Das nordarische (sakische) Lehrgedicht des Buddhismus*[9] which contains, among others, the edition of the Khotanese version of the legend of the juggler Bhadra. It is preserved in fragments only, and, when compared with the Tibetan and Chinese texts, it seems to constitute a free, literary paraphrase of the legend, independent of the text belonging to the *Ratnakūṭa*. Leumann (in the »Anhänge« to his work) gives an abridged translation of the latter[10]. Since he only wished to give the outline of the legend, he omitted many passages (§§ 19—31, 34—74, 76, 79—121, 123—128) in this translation, especially the gāthās and the enumeration of the tetrades, *i. e.* the most important parts of the sūtra from the point of view of doctrine.

---

[5] Ed. by G. Tucci, Mem. della R. Academia Nazionale dei Lincei, vol. XVII, fasc. 1, Roma 1923; by Jiryo Masuda, Journ. of the Taishō Univers., vol. VI—VII, Part II, Tokyo 1930.

[6] Hoernle Mss. n° 143, Sa 17.

[7] *Ms. remains of Bud. Lit. found in East. Turkestan*, pp. 116—121.

[8] *Bodhisattva Prātimokṣa Sūtra*, IHQ, VII, June 1931, n° 2, pp. 259ff (especially pp. 278—285).

[9] Aus dem Nachlaß herausgegeben von Manu Leumann, Abhandlungen für die Kunde des Morgenlandes, XX., Leipzig 1933—1936.

[10] pp. 361—366.

And even for the rest, his translation is abridged and not always reliable[11], as it is based on one T. Ms. only which is not the best, and as it is rarely compared with the Chinese text[12]. For all those reasons a new translation, and especially a critical edition of the full Tibetan text, does not seem superfluous.

2. The *Bhadramāyākāravyākaraṇa* possesses rather a literary value than a doctrinal one[13]. It is one of the texts, so rare in Mahāyāna, which are not overcharged with additions and where the narrative and the doctrinal subjects constitute a logical whole. The anecdotal contents of the sūtra are constituted by the story of the juggler Bhadra who wanted to deceive the Buddha with magical tricks in order to prove that the claim of the Tathāgata to omniscience was false. He created a magical feast in a rubbish hole and invited the Buddha with his monks. The Buddha saw through this stratagem, but performed such a magic that Bhadra could not revoke his charms, was obliged to acknowledge the superiority of the Buddha and was converted.

This theme, *i. e.* the rivalry of two enchanters of which the weaker cannot withdraw his own spells, can be doubtlessly found, with various modifications, in all the literatures of the world, having its echo *e. g.* in the well-known ballad of Goethe »*Der Zauberlehrling*«, and the history of that theme could be made the subject of a special study. In Buddhist writings this legend is known, besides our texts, in two other, probably independent, redactions, *viz.*: in the »Sakian« version, already mentioned, and in the Pali tradition, where reminiscences of that legend are found in the following story from the »Commentary of the *Dhammapada*.«[14]

There lived at Śrāvasti two friends, Sirigutta a Buddhist lay devotee and Garahadinna, a Jain follower. The latter, wishing to convert his friend, praised the omniscience of the Jain teachers. In order to test this omniscience Sirigutta invited those Jain monks to a feast, and secretly dug

---

[11] Cf. foot-notes 164, 371, 630, 648, 672.

[12] Not always without mistakes, cf. foot-notes 38, 86.

[13] It is perhaps the reason why it has not been quoted in later treatises, as far as I could test it.

[14] Norman's ed. I, 2 pp. 435–445. An abridged German translation is given by Leumann, L. pp. 366, 367.

a long ditch between two houses, filled it with dung and mire, drove stumps on its sides and stretched ropes across. He then put seats on the top and stood the front legs of the chairs on the edge of the ditch, whereas the back legs rested on the ropes so that, the moment anybody sat down, he would tip over and be flung into the ditch head downwards. He covered the seats with carpets, took empty vessels, tied over their apertures with rags and banana-leaves, soiled them with rice-milk, lumps of rice, ghee, sugar-juice and bits of cakes, and placed them behind the house.

The following day there came 500 Jain monks. Sirigutta welcomed them, thinking to himself: »If you know everything, you will not enter into my house, because there is no food for You; but if You do not know, You will enter and You will fall into the ditch with dung.« When the monks were ready to be seated, he asked them to sit down all at the same time, in accordance with the custom of the house. At that very moment he ordered the carpets to be pulled off and they all fell into the ditch. Sirugutta jeered at them and ordered them to be sent off.

They ran with laments to Garahadinna who complained to the King claiming a fine of 1000 *kārṣāpaṇas* from Sirigutta. The King, however, after hearing the whole story, condemned Garahadinna and his friends to pay this fine.

Garahadinna then resolved to revenge himself in the same way. He waited for the moment when, in his turn, Sirigutta began to praise the omniscience of his Buddhist teachers, and, »delighted as if someone had scratched his itching spots«, asked him to invite the Buddha with 500 monks to the feast. Sirigutta transmitted this invitation to Buddha, but warned him that it might conceal a subterfuge. In fact Buddha perceived with his supernatural sight that Garahadinna intented to dig a great ditch between two houses, fill it with pieces of acacia-wood, set it on fire and thrust Buddha with the monks upon the glowing embers. Nevertheless, the Buddha decided to accept the invitation and predicted that, at the moment when he put his foot on the ditch with charcoal, large lotus flowers would spring up from the bed of the ditch, and that Buddha and the 500 monks would sit down on their pericarps. Owing to these miracles 84000 persons would attain a full insight into the Truth, Sirigutta and Garahadinna would become converted *(sotāpanna)* and bestow great treasures on the Order.

Garahadinna really made all these preparations, just as Buddha had predicted, covered the glowing charcoal with boards and faggots, glued them up with cowdung, on one side laid out weak planks and awaited the arrival of the Buddha and the monks. In the meantime, a great crowd assembled near his house, the heretics hoping to see the humilation of Buddha and the Buddhist lay devotees wishing to see the mastery of their teacher.

Everything happened as Buddha had predicted. When Garahadinna saw the lotus miracle, he was in despair, for he had no food to entertain his guests. He confessed his lie to Sirigutta and begged him for help. Sirigutta told him to look into the vessels and they were indeed miraculously filled up, so that Garahadinna could satisfy the hunger of Buddha and of the whole Order. On this occasion Buddha uttered two stanzas of the *Dhammapada*[15].

In this Pali version, only the principal subject of the treacherous feast which aimed at confounding the Buddha and which resulted in the conversion of both the deceiver and the persons present, — is preserved. However, as is natural in a Hīnayāna text, the rivalry of the sorcerers is not mentioned, whereas, in the Mahāyāna text, it serves as a pretext to expound the doctrine of the universal *māyā*. In the Pali version a simple Jain devotee takes the place of the sorcerer, and his subterfuge is performed by quite natural means. And, even when Buddha frustrates his intention in a magical way, this miracle is not made use of for doctrinal conclusions.

The Khotanese version agrees with our text much closer, though it is not likely that it has any direct connection with the Sanskrit text. It is a literary, versified paraphrase of the legend, often written in the so called *kāvya* style. From the preserved fragments, the first[16] (stanzas 1—30) corresponds more or less with the §§ 1—5 of our text, but develops far more the details. Bhadra appears here as a member of a plot of heretical leaders, among which Parāśara, Maskarin, Sañjaya and Nirgrantha[17] are named. They intend to confound Buddha owing to whom they are loosing adepts. Almost the entire fragment is devoted to a picturesque and dramatic description of their council. The second fragment, highly characteristic of the *kāvya* style, contains a detailed description of the cemetery where Bhadra magically creates

---

[15] *Dhammapada* 58, 59
Yathā saṃkāradhānasmiṃ ujjhitasmiṃ mahāpathe
padumaṃ tatha jāyetha sucigandhaṃ manoramaṃ
Evaṃ saṃkārabhūtesu andhabhūte puthujjane
atirocate paññāya sammāsambuddhasāvako
The entire story is treated as a commentary to these two stanzas.

[16] L. pp. 7—11.

[17] The author of the Khotanese version links the names of two well-known philosophical leaders from the Buddha's times: Sañjaja Belaṭṭhiputta and Nirgrantha Jñataputra, as the name of one single person Sañjaya Nirgrantha. The mention of Nirgrantha proves that here, like in the Pali version, the intention of deceiving is ascribed to the Jains.

an entertainment for Buddha[18]; further the invitation of Buddha[19] and his discourse with Aniruddha, which corresponds, in our text, with the discourse with Mahāmaudgalyāyana (§ 8—10), but concerns other subjects: instead of the description of the *vāyumaṇḍalas*, it is an instruction about the 3 kinds of *prātihāryas*, where Buddha states that Bhadra is too clever to be subdued by ordinary magic *(ṛddhi-prātihārya);* he must be converted by means of the teaching on the dharma *(dharmadeśanā-prātihārya)*[20]. Further on, this fragment contains a lively description of the arrival of Buddha[21] and of the impression which the arrangement of the feast produced on the assembled guests. In the meantime Śakra throws out the remaining corpses from the cemetery and creates a heavenly throne for the Buddha[22]. Then Bhadra strives to withdraw his spell, but cannot do it[23]. As he is highly perplexed, Vajrapāṇi approaches him and hands him a gong. At the order of Ānanda, Bhadra strikes the gong out of which the *gāthās* praising the power and the omniscience of Buddha resound. Bhadra confesses his sins[24] and asks for forgiveness. The second and last fragment ends with Buddha's lofty words stating that he loves all the creatures as a father and does not feel even the slightest anger toward anybody.

As only 17 stanzas at most are missing till the end of the text, it would be difficult to suppose that they contained any more essential matter. Therefore one can presume that, in all probality, in the Khotanese legend as well, the greatest stress was laid on the action of the legend, and that doctrinal subjects were left in the background.

---

[18] I corresponds with § 11 of our text.

[19] §§ 6, 7 of our text.

[20] Leumann treats it (p. 6) as a proof of the more sublimated character of the Khotanese oversion when compared with other versions where Buddha converts Bhadra by means of ordinary magical tricks, *e. g.* the impossibility to withdraw the charms, the multiplication of his body, etc.

[21] § 16 of our text.

[22] Here we have a reminiscence of a motive which is much more developed in the Sanskrit text (§ 12, 13) where Śakra and the 4 Great Kings create side by side with Bhadra competitive arrangements for the entertainment of Buddha.

[23] § 14 of our text.

[24] § 17 of our text.

3. Thus only in our text, which can be called the Sanskrit version, the legend of Bhadra constitutes a canvas on which doctrinal conclusions are interwoven: moreover, as was mentioned above, these considerations make up a logical whole with the action. In this respect the *Bhadramāyākāravyākaraṇa* shows an exceptional unity of contents which is only interrupted by the enumeration of the tetrades of *dharmas* which are characteristic of the Bodhisattvas (§§ 79—121).

On the whole the doctrinal standpoint of the texts is in agreement with the fundamental theses of the ancient Mahāyāna: the thesis of the *samatā* (cf. §§ 62—67), the thesis of the irreality of the phenomenal world and especially of the Buddha's physical shape (§§ 57—61, 70, 72), the *śūnyavāda* (§§ 25, 73). The greatest stress, however, is laid on the doctrine of *māyā*, the universal illusion. The analogy between the enchanter Bhadra and the universal enchanter Buddha is consistently developed. The Lord, wishing to instruct Bhadra, takes the witchcraft of the latter as a starting point[25]. Bhadra knows that the feast he has created is unreal. Buddha explains to him that not only the magical entertainment but also the persons which enjoy it, whom Bhadra considered to be real, are illusory like the entire world. »Just as the juggler Bhadra creates this arrangement magically, so illusory is the entire reality« — says Prabhāketu (§ 24)[26]. The entire reality and even the person of Buddha are illusory: »The enjoyments and gains of all the beings, Bhadra, are created by the *māyā* of *karman*: this Order of monks is created by the *māyā* of *dharma;* I am created by the *māyā* of *jñāna*, the *trisāhasramahāsāhasralokadhātu* is created by the *māyā* of *viśvābhinirvṛtti,* and all the *dharmas* are created by the *māyā* of *pratyayasaṃbhāra*« (§ 18).

This illusion is a phantasmagory created by Buddha deliberately and on purpose, as Bhadra himself says bluntly after his conversion (§ 134): »The Lord, though there exists no »self«, teaches the Truth using the conventional word »beings«, and,

---

25 It is clearly stated by Maitreya (§ 30) that the *māyā* of Bhadrâ is taken on purpose as a model for pedagogical motives: »just as fire increases by adding oil, so the *māyā* of Buddha becomes manifest owing to the *māyā* of Bhadra« (cf. also § 28).

26 Cf. also § 31 and 55.

though there exists no soul and no individual person, the Lord, when teaching the Truth, adopts the word »person«. Therefore he is a great deceiver. After having reached Enlightenment he does not see any *dharma* which dies, transmigrates or is born, and yet he teaches the doctrine of death, transmigration and rebirth.« The difference between the *māyā* of Buddha and the *māyā* of Bhadra is of two kinds. Firstly it is quantitative: while the magical power of Bhadra applies but to a slight part of reality, is »one-sided« *(ekadeśa)*, the *māyā* of Buddha is universal, and nothing can be compared with it (§§ 8, 28, 35). Secondly the difference is qualitative: the »deceit« of Buddha has a salutary purpose, it leads beings to their supreme aim, it helps them to realize the illusionality of the world. »All the thoughts, even sinful ones, produce the thought directed to Enlightenment« (§ 100). The feast offered by Bhadra, though it had a bad, fraudulous intention, had nevertheless a positive value, because it was a *dāna* bestowed on Buddha[27] and because it gave an opportunity for the conversion of those who were present at it. Therefore Buddha, though he was aware of the deceit, accepted the invitation.

The true and pure *dāna*, however, consists in the realization that the phenomenal world is unreal (§§ 19—22, 29), as Ānanda says (§ 23): »They who are free from mind and body, are themselves the supreme offering«.

A few words should be added concerning Bhadra himself. The name given to the juggler does not seem fortuitous. In the Buddhist tradition the names Bhadra or its variant Subhadra are connected with the spreaders of schisms and doubts In the Southern tradition we find a legend (in the *Mahāparinibbānasutta*, *Dīgha-Nik.* II, p. 162 and in the *Cullavagga* p. 284, 285) which relates that, when the monks were lamenting Buddha's recent

---

[27] Thus the fact that Bhadra cannot withdraw his spell becomes symbolical, cf. the words of Śakra in § 15: »Bhadra, just as Thou art not able to annihilate the arrangement of this place settled for the sake of the Tathāgata, so, if any man conceives whatever thought directed to the Thathāgata, that thought cannot be withdrawn, and will be the inner cause of his future *parinirvāṇa.*«

These conceptions found their full developement in the cult of Amitābha whose name, uttered even in blasphemy, warranted rebirth in paradise.

death, one of them, Subhadda by name, stood up in the assembly and cried: »Do not grieve, we are now delivered from the Great *Śramaṇa* who oppressed us saying: ‚this beseems ye' and ‚that beseems ye not!' Now we shall do what we like, and we shall not do what we do not like.« These words, so dangerous for the keeping up of the unity and the continuity of Buddhist tradition, were one of the reasons for which Mahākassapa insisted on calling the Council.

These facts come out still more distinctly in the Northern tradition where (*Tāranātha* 52, 298) a certain monk called Bhadra is mentioned. He is considered as an incarnation of Māra. When he became a Buddhist monk, in the year 137 of Nirvāṇa, he undertook to find out all doubtful points and contradictions in the Scriptures. As consequence, a whole series of various opinions arose, and the dissensions kept on increasing, as a growing number of monks fell under the influence of the Evil One. Bhadra's real nature was not found out till after his death.

Considering that, in the above story, Bhadra appears as the continuator of another spreader of troubles Mahādeva, Kern's opinion (*Geschiedenis van het Buddhisme,* II, p. 292) that in the Buddhist tradition both these figures represent Śiva, the god of destruction, has some foundation, since we are aware that both Bhadra and Mahādeva are names for Śiva.

As it was stated above, the §§ 79 – 121 are unconnected with the principal subject of the sūtra. They contain the enumeration of the *dharmas* which characterize a Boddhisattva Those *dharmas* are classified in groups each containing four elements, but this classification corresponds rarely to the four-fold schemes known from elsewhere, *e. g.* from the *Aṅguttara-Nikāya*, and gives the impression of being a rather arbitrary bringing together of four divergent elements It often happens that the collective title of a group has not much in common with the elements constituting the group. This mode of classification in tetrades is very characteristic of the texts of that kind, cf. the *Kāśyapaparivarta*, the *Rāṣṭrapālaparipṛcchā*, the *Bodhisattvabhūmi*, the XXIIIrd chpt. of the *Samādhirājasūtra*, etc.

The *dharmas* enumerated in the §§ 79—121 belong mostly to the category of practical features or duties of the Bodhisattvas.

The following points may be noted: (§ 91) »Love Thy neighbour as Thyself!«; (§ 114) »Rely on the meaning and not on the letter; rely on the teaching and not on the man«; (§ 117) »contradict not when anyone else expounds the *dharma*«; (§ 120) »no treachery!«; (§ 121) »he who is endowed with skilfulness, can accumulate on one Perfection all the remaining Perfections; if he knows the nature of one being, he can conceive the nature of all beings; if he realizes one kind of pure *dharma*, he may realize all the pure *dharmas*; and if he has reached the *dharmatā*, he may believe in all the Buddhas through one Buddha.«

4. The edition of a Buddhist text which is not preserved in an Indian original should, in my opinion, be composed of 3 parts:

1. the critical edition of the Tibetan text (eventually that of the Mongolian one as well; the edition of the Chinese versions is not indispensable, for those texts are already published in the Taishō ed.),

2. the translation into a European language, and

3. the Tib.-Chinese index (which may also contain equivalents of other languages, if corresponding versions exist). Such an index could to a certain extent render the reconstruction of the Sanskrit-Chinese equivalents possible.

The utility of the 1st and 3rd part needs not be proved But I consider also the 2nd part as indispensable, because it makes up for the reconstruction of the lost original. The reconstruction into Sanskrit is a rather useless amusement, and is seldom successful not only with European, but also with Indian Sanskritists. On the contrary a manner of translating which by analogy with the »critical edition« may be called a »critical translation«, would come nearest to the original. The Tibetan version must doubtlessly be chosen as the base of such a translation as it follows most accurately the original text. But sometimes this version is also deceiving and, in certain cases, the Chinese translation is more correct. In such instances the »critical translation« should be based rather on the Chinese text, but all the deviations from the adopted redaction which occur in other versions should be indicated in the foot-notes. Just as in the »critical apparatus« all the »variae lectiones«, even the obvious mistakes, are noted, so all the »variae versiones«[28], even sheer absurdities, should be i[...] (under the text) in a critical translation of this kind. In [...] manner, not only all the data helping to reconstruct the origi[...] become synthetized (even those which though they seem absur[...] at first sight, may, after a thorough investigation, prove to be correct), but also this assemblage of different versions may constitute a useful contribution to the study of the technique of Buddhist translators. Therefore such an »apparatus« is desirable as well in texts with which the original has been preserved. The comparison of this original with all the types of translations supplies valuable material for cases where there is only one version at our disposal: the Tibetan or especially the Chinese.

Till now this task was exclusively fulfilled by indexes. But the form of indexes is too rigid and laconic to pay enough attention to phraseological equivalents. Moreover we often do not find equivalents, but misunderstandings. Even in such good indexes as *e. g.* Rosenberg's *Dictionnary* often quite incongruous comparisons are met with. It results from the method resorted to. When, in two parallel passages, two expressions are found which correspond with each other in a sentence, these expressions are noted as equivalent even when the proper meanings of those words have very little in common. These discrepancies are interpreted as the result of the artificial character of Buddhist translations and as a proof that there existed no fixed Buddhist terminology in Chinese, whereas they very often consitute divergences made on purpose or simply misreadings. Side by side with sheer misreadings like *karṇa* instead of *varṇa* (§ 135)[29], there occur subtler cases as *e. g.* the rendering of *pañcacakṣuḥ*, in Chinese, by *hui yen*[30]. We have here neither a »pars pro toto«, nor a free interpretation of the term, but simply a confusion of *pañca°* with *prajñā°* which resemble each other, especially in their Middle Indian forms. Similarly *śraddhā* is often translated as *ch'ing ching*,

---

[28] Of course, not slight phraseological or stylistic divergences but essential differences are concerned.

[29] Cf. foot-note 665. This case proves besides that even expert Chinese translators did not mind if their translation contained nonsenses.

[30] Cf. foot-notes 74, 318.

on the contrary *śuddha* rendered by *hsin*[31]. Here also *śuddha* l *śraddhā* are misread and confused. Cf. also confusions as *ṣṭyaṅgopeta* and *aṣṭāṅgopeta* (note 98), *praṇidhāna* and *pratibhāna* ıote 277), *akṣara* and *akṣaya* (note 570), *karaṇḍa* and *karaṇa*(?) note 107), *anuśaṃsa* and *anukampa* (note 282), etc. These cases, difficult to be discussed in an index, are best dealt with in the foot-notes of the translation. Such an »apparatus« must note those cases and, when possible, explain the mistake. But even if an explanation cannot be found, those facts must be brought into evidence in the notes, for they can serve as materials for comparison in other analogical cases.

5. There exist 1 Tibetan and 2 Chinese translations of the *Bhadramāyākāravyākaraṇa*. The Tibetan text is supplied with the following colophon:

rgya-gar-gyi mkhan-po 'dzi-na-mi tra daṅ / pra-jña-var-ma[32] *daṅ / źu-chen-gyi lo-tsa-ba ban-de ye-śes-sde la-sogs*[33]*-pas bsgyur-ciṅ źus-te gtan-la phab-pa /*

The translators mentioned in this colophon: Jinamitra, Prajñāvarma and Ye-śes-sde worked in the IXth century A. D.[34]. For my edition I have used three recensions of that text, the Ms. of the Staatsbibliothek in Berlin[35] and the xylographs of the Peking and Narthang ed. from the Bibliothèque Nationale of Paris.

Bhadramāyākāravyākaraṇa (sgyu-ma-mkhan bzaṅ-po luṅ-bstan-pa) constitutes the n° 21 of the *Ratnakūṭa (dkon-brtsegs-pa)* section and is contained in the:

B. Ms. of Berlin, n° 51,1 in the catalogue of Beckh — ff. 1—27
N. Narthang ed. Bibl. Nat. Paris, fonds tib. 404 — Ca 3°, ff. $74b^{5}$—$100a^{3}$
P. Peking ed. Bibl. Nat. Paris, fonds tib. 54 — Zi 1°, ff. 1—$22a^{1}$

B and P show a very close agreement[36], N differs from both and contains the best and the most correct readings. But

---

31 Cf. foot-note 199, 200 and R. foot-note 96.

32 The Peking edition has *va-jra-va-rma.*

33 All the texts: *stsogs.*

34 Cf. Feer, *Annales du Mus. Guimet* II, p. 113.

35 This Ms. was the basis of the above mentioned abridged translation of Leumann.

36 P. Pelliot, already in 1914 *(Notes à propos d'un Catalogue du Kanjur,* JA, juill. août 1914, p. 115) expressed the supposition that the

the first Tibetan redaction, on which all those texts were founded, was not free from errors as it can be proved by the faulty readings, common to all the redactions, which may be corrected only with the help of the Chinese translation, *e. g. thams* in the § 50[37]. In general the style of this translation is often intricate, and, especially in the *gāthās*, it has a very irregular syntax. In those cases, a literal translation into English would result in absurdities. Therefore, especially as the leading thought is usually clear and simple, I did not strive, in such cases, to render the construction of the Tibetan sentence accurately, but based the translation on the meaning obtained by comparing the passage with the Chinese versions. I have translated clearly against the Tibetan text (and in accordance with the Chinese version or common sense) only a few passages, where there is no doubt that the Tibetan translation is wrong (see notes 98, 153, 181, 195, 224, 242, 243, 326, 358, 462, 525, 531, 586).

The Chinese translations of our text bear the following titles: Ch_1. (Taishō 324, XII, ff. 31a–37a) *Huan shih jen hsien ching* and Ch_2. (Taishō 310 (21), XI, ff. 486b—492b) *Shou huan shih po-t'o-lo chi hui*[38].

The first version is attributed to Dharmarakṣa (Chu-fa-hu) from the Western Chin dynasty who worked at translations between 266 and 317 A. D. It is really an archaic version which is characterized not only by an inappropriate and awkward use of technical terms, but also by frequent misunderstandings and misreadings. On the other hand, this translation is less laconic than Ch_2 and, in spite of numerous errors, is more helpful

---

Ms. of Berlin «dérive en réalite non pas de l'édition de Derge, mais d'une recension apparentée aux recensions pékinoises et que je suis malheureusement hors d'état de déterminer«. Also Marcelle Lalou points out the agreement between B and P in the arrangement of the materials (*La version tibétaine du Ratnakūṭa*, JA, oct. dec. 1927, p. 244). My work allows to corroborate this agreement also in details.

[37] Cf. foot-note 268 and also 108, 436 and 616.

[38] Leumann mentions (p. 361) one more Chinese text (Taishō 1378), which he calls »ein kurzes sūtra, das die von Bhadra gesprochene Mantras behandelt«. In fact this is a very short text where Bhadra utters a certain number of spells but, besides his person, the sūtra has nothing in common with the *Bhadramāyākāravyākaraṇa*.

in the reconstruction of the original and has sometimes preserved the best reading[39].

Ch_2 is the work of Bodhiruci of the T'ang dynasty, which was done between 693 and 713 A. D. This is the most intelligent translation, but a rather laconic one, rendering the essential thoughts only and, especially in the *gāthās*, neglecting the details[40].

In some respects both Chinese translations seem more correct than the Tibetan version, *e. g.* in the use of the appelations *śramaṇa Gautama* and *Bhagavat*[41], *māyākāra* and *kulaputra*[42].

But these differences are concerned with details only. In size and and in the disposition of subjects, all the versions are practically identical so that we can state in all confidence that from the IIIrd century (date of the first translation) till the IXth century (date of the Tibetan version) the text underwent no alterations and that, consequently, the form which we try to reconstruct on the basis of all the versions corresponds to the original text which must have been composed before the IIIrd century, probably not much later than the *Kāśyapaparivarta.*

I am responsible for the division of the text into §§. In order to facilitate research, I have added at the end a tabulated list of the corresponding paragraphs in the Chinese texts of Taishō. It has a special importance for the prose passages and several *gāthās*, where the Taishō ed. gives a wrong division. *E. g.* in the §§ 34—74, in Ch_1, each stanza has to contain 8 quadrisyllables and not 6, as it is divided in Taishō.

A detailed Tibetan-Chinese index will appear later on as a separate fascicle.

6. In am quite conscious that my edition and translation do not fulfil all the demands which I myself make in the case of such a work, and I do not claim to have overcome all the difficulties. I consider that many problems involved in this work

---

[39] Cf. *e. g.* notes 47, 98, 116, 266, 585.

[40] Sometimes however it is more detailed than the original, e. g. when, instead of translating the term *īryāpatha*, it analyzes it, enumerating the 4 kinds of behaviour, see note 142, cf. also notes 131, 194, etc.

[41] Cf. notes 90, 104, 179.

[42] Cf. notes 383, 628.

cannot be solved beyond all doubts with the materials we have at our disposal though some might probably be solved by scholars more skilled and expert than myself. I hope to find indulgence for my errors, as I have had to work at an almost novel task. In many cases I was aware that all the three texts on which I based my translation were corrupt, but, as I could not find the right emendation, I was obliged to translate those passages literally, limiting myself to assembling in the foot-notes all the available data which could help those who would see a better way to find a solution.

I avail myself of the opportunity to acknowledge my indebtedness to all those who were kind enough to help me in my work. My gratitude is due above all to Professor St. Schayer for the active interest he took in the publication of this volume and the valuable help he rendered me in my work. I am also very much obliged to Mademoiselle Marcelle Lalou who very kindly helped me to look for some data which were inaccessible to me, assisted me with her profound knowledge of the Tibetan language and was kind enough to read the proofs. I owe moreover the deepest gratitude to all the persons whose suggestions allowed me to solve many difficult problems of my work, especially to Professor P. Demiéville and to Professor Jean Przyluski.

Last but not least I have to thank the authorities of the Fundusz Kultury Narodowej whose kind help allowed me to bring my work to an end.

Constantin Régamey

List of abbreviations

Γ : The Tibetan version of the *Bhadramāyākāravyākaraṇa* contained in 3 recensions:

B : Ms. of Berlin, N 51,1 FF. ff. 1–27.

N : xylogr. of the Bibl. Nationale Paris, fonds tib. 404, ff. 74 b[5]–100 a[3]

P : xylogr. of the Bibl. Nationale Paris, fonds tib. 54, ff. 1–22 a[1]

Ch : The Chinese version of the *Bhadramāyākāravyākaraṇa, viz.:*

Ch : Taishō 324 (XII, ff. 31 a–37 a)

Ch : Taishō 310(21) (XI, ff. 486 b–492 b)

c. Ch : emendation according the Chinese version.

ad. : adds.

ins. : inserts.

om. : omits.

* * *

AK : *Abhidharmakośa*, translation of Louis de La Vallée Poussin, Paris Louvain, 1923–31.

IHQ : *Indian Historical Quarterly*, Calcutta.

JA : *Journal Asiatique*, Paris.

JRAS : *Journal of the Royal Asiatic Society*, London.

L. : E. Leumann, *Das nordarische (sakische) Lehrgedicht des Buddhismus*, Abhandlungen für die Kunde des Morgenlandes, XX, Nr. 1, Leipzig 1933–36.

Mhv. : *Mahāvyutpatti*, ed. Sakaki, Kyoto 1916.

OLZ : *Orientalistische Literaturzeitung*, Leipzig.

Pr. P. : E. Obermiller, *The Doctrine of Prajñā-pāramitā*, Acta Orientalia, XI, 1932.

R. : K. Régamey, *Three Chapters from the Samādhirājasūtra*, Publications of the Oriental Commission of the Warsaw Society of Sciences and Letters, nº 1, Warsaw 1938.

TIBETAN TEXT

rgya-gar skad-du / ā-rya[1]-bha-dra[2]-mā-yā-kā-ra[3]-vya-ka[4]-ra-ṇa nā-ma ma-hā-yā-na[5]-sū-tra / bod skad-du / 'phags-pa[6] sgyu-ma-mkhan bzaṅ-po luṅ-bstan-pa źes bya-ba theg-pa chen-po'i mdo /[7]

/ saṅs-rgyas daṅ byaṅ-chub-sems-dpa' thams-cad-la phyag 'tshal-lo /

1. 'di skad bdag-gis thos-pa / dus gcig-na[8] bcom-ldan-'das rgyal-po'i khab-na bya-rgod-kyi[9] phuṅ-po'i ri-la / dge-sloṅ stoṅ-ñis-brgya-lṅa-bcu'i dge-sloṅ-gi dge-'dun chen-po daṅ / byaṅ-chub-sems-dpa' sems-dpa'-chen-po mṅon-par-grags-pa / mṅon-par-śes-pa-thob-pa / gzuṅs-thob-pa / rdzu-'phrul-gyi cho-'phrul-thob-pa / mi-skye-ba'i chos-la bzod-pa-thob-pa lṅa-stoṅ-la 'di-lta-ste / byaṅ-chub-sems-dpa' sems-dpa'-chen-po seṅ-ge daṅ / byaṅ-chub-sems-dpa' sems-dpa'-chen-po seṅ-ge-blo-gros daṅ / byaṅ... sems... tsan-dan-bzaṅ-po daṅ / byaṅ... sems... kha-lo-sgyur[10]-ba daṅ / byaṅ... sems... kha-lo-sgyur[10]-ba-chen-po daṅ / byaṅ... sems... 'od-dpal daṅ / byaṅ... sems... 'od-byed daṅ / byaṅ... sems... 'od-gzi-brjid[11]-daṅ-ldan źiṅ ṅa-ro-sñan-pa daṅ / byaṅ... sems... 'od-bkod-pa daṅ / byaṅ... sems... blo-gsal[12] daṅ / byaṅ... sems... sems-can-gyi sñiṅ-po daṅ / byaṅ... sems... sems-can-kha-lo-sgyur[10]-ba dul-ba-daṅ-ldan-pa daṅ[13] / byams-pa-la sogs[14]-pa bskal[15]-pa-bzaṅ-po'i byaṅ-chub-sems-dpa' sems-dpa'-chen-po thams-cad daṅ / 'jam-dpal gźon-nur-gyur-pa daṅ / de-dag-la sogs[14]-pa byaṅ-chub-sems-dpa' sems-dpa'-chen-po lṅa-stoṅ daṅ / thabs-gcig[16]-tu bźugs-te / lha-rnams-kyi dbaṅ-po brgya-byin daṅ yaṅ thabs-gcig[16]-go / mi-mjed-kyi bdag-po tshaṅs-pa daṅ yaṅ thabs-gcig[16]-go / rgyal-po chen-po bźi daṅ yaṅ thabs-gcig[16]-go / lha daṅ klu daṅ gnod-sbyin daṅ /

---

[1] BN *om.* ā-rya [2] BN bhad-dra [3] B rya [4] N kā [5] N ya-nā [6] BN *om.* 'phags-pa [7] N *ad.* bam-po thag-ma gcig [8] P *om.* na [9] N *om.* kyi [10] N bsgyur [11] N brjed [12] N *ad.* pa [13] N *om.* [14] BP stsogs [15] N skal [16] P cig

lha-ma-yin daṅ / nam-mkha'-ldiṅ daṅ / dri-za daṅ / mi-'am-ci daṅ / lto-'phye[1]-chen-po daṅ du-mas kyaṅ yoṅs-su-bskor-to //

2. de-nas bcom-ldan-'das ni rgyal-po'i khab-kyi groṅ-khyer chen-po-la brten[2]-ciṅ bźugs-te / rgyal-po daṅ blon-po-chen-po-rnams daṅ / bram-ze daṅ / khyim-bdag daṅ / groṅ-rdal daṅ / ljoṅs-kyi mi-rnams-kyis ni gus-par byas / bla-mar byas / bsñen-bkur byas / mchod-par[3]-byas-so // bcom-ldan-'das-kyis chos-gos daṅ / źal-zas daṅ / gzims-cha daṅ / gdan daṅ / sñun-gsos daṅ / sman-zoṅ ni brñes /

3. bcom-ldan-'das-kyi grags-pa daṅ / sñan-pa daṅ / tshigs-su-bcad-pa rgya-chen-po ni mṅon-par-'phags-te / 'di-lta[4]-ste de-bźin-gśegs-pa / dgra-bcom-pa / yaṅ-dag-par-rdzogs-pa'i saṅs-rgyas / rig-pa-daṅ-źabs[5]-su-ldan-pa / bde-bar-gśegs-pa / 'jig-rten-mkhyen-pa / skyes-bu-'dul-ba'i kha-lo-sgyur-ba / bla-na-med-pa / lha daṅ mi-rnams-kyi ston-pa / saṅs-rgyas bcom-ldan-'das de ni thams-cad-mkhyen-pa / thams-cad gzigs-pa-daṅ-ldan-pa-ste / thams-cad ni mkhyen[6] / thams-cad ni gzigs / de-bźin-gśegs-pa'i stobs-bcu-daṅ-ni-ldan / de-bźin-gśegs-pa'i mi-'jigs[7]-pa-bźi-daṅ-ni-ldan / so-so-yaṅ-dag-par-rig-pa-bźi-daṅ-ni-ldan / saṅs-rgyas-kyi chos ma-'dres-pa bco-brgyad[8]-daṅ-ni-ldan / byams-pa-chen-po-daṅ-ni-ldan[9] / sñiṅ-rje-chen-po-daṅ-ni-ldan / saṅs-rgyas-kyi spyan-ñams-pa-mi-mna'-ba-daṅ-ni-ldan / spyan-lṅa-daṅ-ni-ldan / cho-'phrul yaṅ brñes-te / kun-brjod-pa'i cho-'phrul ni brñes / rjes-su-bstan-pa'i cho-'phrul ni brñes / rdzu-'phrul-gyi cho-'phrul ni brñes-so[10] / bźed-na stoṅ-gsum-gyi stoṅ-chen-po'i 'jig-rten-gyi khams groṅ-khyer-daṅ-bcas-pa / groṅ-rdal-daṅ-bcas-pa / sa-daṅ-bcas-pa / 'gro-ba-daṅ-bcas-pa[11] / ri-rab-daṅ-bcas-pa / rgya-mtsho'i mtha'[12]-gtugs-pa / lha'i gnas-daṅ-bcas-pa[13] / khor-yug-daṅ 'obs-su-bcas-pa / rtsba-daṅ-śiṅ-daṅ-rir-bcas-pa 'di nam-mkha'-la bskal-pa'am[14] / bskal-pa-las lhag-par skra'i rtse-mo'i cha-śas-kyis 'dzin-par mdzad-do //

4. yaṅ de'i tshe rgyal-po'i khab-kyi groṅ-khyer chen-po-na sgyu-ma-mkhan bzaṅ-po źes bya-ba bstan-bcos-la śin-tu-mkhas-pa gsaṅ-sṅags[15]-la śin-tu-mkhas-pa bzo-daṅ-rig-pa-la mkhas[16]-pa las-kyi mtha' byas-zin-pa rab-tu-byed-pa byas-pa sgra-grags-pa / yul

---

[1] B phye [2] P rten [3] BP pa [4] P ltar [5] P bźabs [6] B *ad.* pa [7] BP 'jig [8] B brgya [9] N *om.* ni-ldan [10] B rdzu-'phrul ni brñes-so [11] N *om.* 'gro-ba-daṅ-bcas-pa [12] N mthas [13] BP *om.* pa [14] B *om.* pa [15] P bsṅags [16] BP 'byam

ma-ga[1]-dhā[2]-na sgyu-ma-mkhan-nam[3] / sgyu-ma-mkhan-gyi slob-ma ji-sñed-pa de-gag-gi mchog-tu-grags-pa / phul-du-grags-pa / źig-gnas-te / des yul ma-ga[1]-dhā[2] ril-gyi[4] skye[5]-bo'i tshogs thams-cad 'dun-par byas[6] / rmoṅs-par byas / mgo-'khor-bar byas-nas ya-mtshan-gyi chos-la bkod-de / bden-pa mthoṅ-ba-rnams daṅ / dad-pa daṅ chos-kyis[7] rjes-su-'braṅ-ba-rnams daṅ / dge-bsñen[8] daṅ / dge-bsñen[8]-ma-rnams ni ma-gtogs-so // des sgyu-mas rmoṅs-par-byed-pa'i rig-pa'i stobs-bskyed-pas rñed-pa daṅ / bkur-sti[9] daṅ / tshigs-su-bcad-pa yaṅ lhag-par-rñed-do //

5. sgyu-ma-mkhan bzaṅ-pos / bcom-ldan-'das-kyi grags-pa daṅ / sñan-pa daṅ / tshigs-su-bcad-pa lhag-par mṅon-par-'phags-te / 'di-ltar de-bźin-gśegs-pa dgra-bcom-pa yaṅ-dag-par-rdzogs-pa'i saṅs-rgyas rig-pa-daṅ-źabs-su-ldan-pa[10].... skra'i rtse-mo'i cha-śas tsam-la 'dzin-par mdzad-do / źes thos-so // thos-nas kyaṅ yaṅ de 'di-sñam-du sems-te / yul ma-ga[1]-dhā[2] ril[11]-gyi skye-bo'i tshogs[12] thams-cad bdag-gis 'dun-par byas / rmoṅs-par byas / mgo-'khor-bar byas-nas / ya-mtshan-gyi chos-la bkod-de / bram[13]-ze daṅ khyim-bdag chen-po gaṅ-dag yin-pa de-dag kyaṅ bdag-gi[14] miṅ-gis rab-tu-mgu-bar gyur-na / de-bźin-gśegs-pa / dgra-bcom-pa / yaṅ-dag-par-rdzogs-pa'i saṅs-rgyas de gcig-pu[15] da-duṅ ma-bgams / rmoṅs-par-ma-byas / mgo-'khor[16]-bar ma-byas-kyis ma-la bdag de-bźin-gśegs-pa dgra-bcom-pa yaṅ-dag-par-rdzogs-pa'i saṅs-rgyas ga-la-ba-der 'gro-bar bya'o // soṅ-nas kyaṅ bgam[17]-par bya-ste / gal-te rmoṅs-pa'am mgo-'khor-bar-bya nus-pa lta-na / de-lta-na yul ma-ga[1]-dhā[2] thams-cad bdag gcig-tu-'dul-lam[18] / bdag-gi rñed-pa daṅ / bkur-sti yaṅ chos-stobs-daṅ-ldan-par 'gyur-ro sñam-mo //

6. de-nas yaṅ sgyu-ma-mkhan bzaṅ-po sṅon-gyi dge-ba'i rtsa-bas bskul[19]-ba daṅ / saṅs-rgyas-kyi mthus rgyal-po'i khab-kyi groṅ-khyer chen-po-nas byuṅ-ste / bya-rgod-kyi phuṅ-po'i ri ga[20]-la-ba daṅ / bcom-ldan-'das ga-la-ba der soṅ-ṅo / soṅ-nas kyaṅ sgyu-ma-mkhan bzaṅ-pos / de-bźin-gśegs-pa ñi-ma bye-ba-phrag 'bum-pas[21] lhag-pa'i 'od-zer 'bar-ba źal zla-ba bye-ba-phrag 'bum-pas[22] lhag-par dri-ma-med-pa sku śiṅ nya[22]-gro-dha'i[23] rgyal-po ltar chu-

---

[1] B gha [2] B ta [3] N *om.* sgyu-ma-mkhan-nam [4] P kyi [5] B sgye [6] N *ad.* pa [7] B kyi [8] P sñen [9] N bsti [10] *As above*, § 3 [11] B yul [12] BP *om.* tshogs [13] B braṅ [14] B gis [15] BN bu [16] P mkhor [17] N 'gam [18] N gcig-tu-'dus [19] P bsgul [20] B rig [21] BP 'bum-bas byams-pas [22] B na [23] BN da'i

źeṅ-gab-pa / mdzod-spu nor-bu dri-ma-med-pa'i 'od-dag-pa ltar gsal-ba / spyan pad-ma daṅ / ud-pa-la sṅon-po kha-'bye-ba / lta-bu'i bkrag yod-pa / spyi-gtsug tshaṅs-pas kyaṅ bltar mi-mthoṅ-ba / 'khor-gyi naṅ-du[1] gsuṅ-dbyaṅs yan-lag-drug-cu[2]-daṅ-ldan-pas / chos ston-pa mthoṅ-ṅo / mthoṅ-nas kyaṅ de'i[3] sku de-lta-bu mthoṅ // gsuṅ-gi phrin-las de-lta-bu thos-nas sems dad-par-gyur-ciṅ de 'di-sñam-du sems-te / ma-la bdag-gis 'di ci thams-cad-mkhyen-la thams-cad[4]-gzigs-pa-daṅ-ldan-pa źig yin-nam 'on-te ma-yin bgam-par-bya gor-ma-chag sñam-mo //

7. de-nas yaṅ[5] sgyu-ma-mkhan bzaṅ-pos / bcom-ldan-'das-kyi źabs-la mgo[6]-bos phyag-'tshal-nas / bgam-pa'i bsam-pas saṅ-gi gdugs tshod-la spyan-'dren-to / źes gsol-to / 'di sñam-du yaṅ sems-te / ci 'dis bdag-gi sems śes-sam 'on-te mi-śes źig-gu / gal-te śes-na ni der 'oṅ-bar mi-'gyur-ro / ci[7]-ste mi-śes-na ni de[8]-na 'oṅ-bar-'gyur-ro sñam-mo // de-nas bcom-ldan-'das-kyis sgyu-ma-mkhan bzaṅ-po gdul-ba'i dbaṅ-du yaṅ mdzad / rgyal-po'i khab-kyi groṅ-khyer chen-po'i skye-bo-phal-po-che gdul-ba'i dbaṅ-du yaṅ mdzad[9]-nas / de[10]-mkhyen bźin-du sgyu-ma-mkhan bzaṅ-po-la dge-sloṅ-gi dge-'dun daṅ bcas-te caṅ-mi-gsuṅ-bas gnaṅ-bar mdzad-do // de-nas yaṅ sgyu-ma-mkhan bzaṅ-po 'di sñam-du sems-te / 'di bdag rnam-par-tho-btsam-pa'i bsam-pa-daṅ-ldan-pa-la / 'dir khas-len-pa daṅ sbyar-na / 'di ni thams-cad-mkhyen-pa yaṅ ma-yin-la / thams-cad-gzigs-pa-daṅ-ldan-pa yaṅ ma-yin-no sñam-mo[11] // de-nas sgyu-ma-mkhan bzaṅ-pos[12] bcom-ldan-'das-kyi źabs-la mgo-bos phyag-'tshal-nas / bcom-ldan-'das-kyi thad-nas soṅ-ṅo //

8. de-nas bcom-ldan-'das-la / tshe-daṅ-ldan-pa mo-'u[13]-dgal-gyi-bu-chen-pos 'di-skad ces gsol-to // sgyu-ma-mkhan bzaṅ-pos ni sgyu-ma'i za-ma-tog-gis dge-sloṅ-gi dge-'dun 'di-la tho-'tsham[14]-par-'gyur-ba[15] lags-so // bcom-ldan-'das-kyis bka'-stsal-pa / mo'u[13]-dgal-gyi-bu khyod sñiṅ-las ma[16]-chuṅ-bar-gyis śig-daṅ / ṅas yun-riṅ-po-nas spyad-pa-bsgrubs-pas-na de-bźin-gśegs-pa ni 'dir dus-mkhyen-pa yin-te / de-bźin-gśegs-pa-la ni lha daṅ bcas-pa'i 'jig-rten-gyis kyaṅ tho-'tsham[17]-par mi-nus-so // mo'u[13]-dgal-gyi-bu gźan yaṅ 'dod-chags ni tho-'tsham-par byed-pa-yin / źe-sdaṅ ni

---

[1] N na [2] P bcu [3] N des [4] B *om.* cad [5] N *om.* [6] P go [7] BP ji [8] BP des [9] P mdzod [10] N *om.* [11] BP nas [12] BP po [13] BP me'u [14] P 'tshams [15] BP *om.* [16] c. Ch., T. *om.* [17] BP btsam

tho-'tsham-par byed-pa-yin / gti[1]-mug ni tho-'tsham-par byed-pa yin[2]-na / de-dag ni de-bźin-gśegs-pas[3] bag-la-ñal daṅ bcas-te zad-bral[4] yoṅs-su-gyur / gzod-ma-nas ma-skyes-pa'i chos-can yin-te / des-na[5] de-bźin-gśegs-pa-la lha daṅ bcas-pa'i 'jig-rten-gyis kyaṅ mtho-'tsham[6]-par mi-nus-so // mo'u[7]-dgal-gyi-bu gźan yaṅ sgyu-ma-mkhan bzaṅ-po'i sgyu-ma ni phyogs-gcig-pa yin-pas sgyu-ma yaṅ-dag-pa ma-yin-gyi / de-bźin-gśegs-pa'i sgyu-ma ni yaṅ-dag-pa[8] yin-te / des[9]-na chos thams-cad sgyu-ma lta-bur mṅon-par-rdzogs-par saṅs-rgyas-so // mo'u[7]-dgal-gyi-bu sems-can-gyi khams-su gdags-par 'dogs-pa ji-sñed-pa de-dag thams-cad 'di-lta-ste / sgyu-ma-mkhan bzaṅ-po'i sgyu-ma 'di-lta-bu-daṅ-ldan-par-gyur kyaṅ de-dag thams-cad-kyis de-bźin-gśegs-pa'i sgyu-ma-la brgya'i char yaṅ ñe-bar-mi-'gro / stoṅ-gi char yaṅ ñe-bar-mi-'gro / bye-ba 'bum-gyi char yaṅ graṅs-su yaṅ / char yaṅ / bgraṅ-bar yaṅ / dper yaṅ / ñe-bar-mi-'gro'o //

9. mo'u[7]-dgal-gyi-bu 'di ji-sñam-du sems / sgyu-ma-mkhan bzaṅ-pos stoṅ-gsum-gyi stoṅ-chen-po'i 'jig-rten-gyi khams 'di rgyan thams-cad-kyis brgyan-par kun-tu-ston nus-sam // gsol-pa / ma[10]-lags-so // bcom-ldan-'das-kyis bka'-stsal-pa / de-bźin-gśegs-pa ni bźed-na 'jig-rten-gyi khams gaṅ-ga'i kluṅ-gi bye-ma sñed brgyan-ciṅ / de-dag[11] thams-cad kyaṅ skra'i rtse-mo'i cha-śas-tsam-la kun-tu-ston-par mdzad kyaṅ / de-bźin-gśegs-pa'i sgyu-ma ril-gyis bstan[12]-par[13] mi-'gyur-ro // mo'u-dgal-gyi-bu phyogs-bcu-na rluṅ-gi dkyil-'khor gaṅ-dag yod-pa 'di-lta-ste / rluṅ-gi dkyil-'khor rnam-par-'thor-byed ces bya-ba daṅ / rluṅ-gi dkyil-'khor yoṅs-su-gcod-byed ces bya-ba gaṅ-dag-gis[14] / stoṅ-gsum-gyi stoṅ-chen-po'i 'jig-rten-gyi khams 'di yoṅs-su-gcod-par-byed-ciṅ / yoṅs-su-bcad-nas kyaṅ 'jig-par-byed-pa daṅ / rluṅ-gi dkyil-'khor kun-tu-'thor-byed daṅ / rnam-par-'thor-byed ces bya-ba 'jig-rten-gyi bar-na rgyu-ba gaṅ-dag yin-pa daṅ / rluṅ-gi dkyil-'khor kun-nas-yoṅs-su-'jog-pa źes bya-ba srid-pa'i rtse-mo-na rgyu-ba gaṅ-dag yin-pa daṅ / rluṅ-gi dkyil-'khor rnam-par-'jig-pa źes bya-ba ri'i rgyal-po ri-rab kyaṅ rnam-par-'jig-par byed-na / ri phal-pa lta-smos kyaṅ ci-dgos-pa gaṅ-dag yin-pa daṅ / rluṅ-gi dkyil-'khor 'bar-byed ces bya-ba sreg-pa'i bskal[15]-pa'i tshe-ldaṅ źiṅ gaṅ-gis-na / me-lce de-dag tshaṅs-

[1] P ti [2] N *om.* pa yin [3] N pa-la [4] N gral [5] P de-na, B de-nas *and om. the words which follow down to* ma-yin-gyi [6] BP brtsam [7] BP me'u [8] B par [9] P de [10] B *om.* [11] N *om.* [12] BP stan [13] N *ad.* ni [14] B dgis [15] N skal

pa'i 'jig-rten-gyi bar-du 'phen-par-byed-pa daṅ / rluṅ-gi dkyil-'khor rnam-par-sgrub-byed ces bya-ba gaṅ-gis sreg[1]-pa'i bskal-pa'i me de źi-bar-byed-pa daṅ / rluṅ-gi dkyil-'khor rab-tu-tshim-byed ces bya-ba[2] gaṅ-gis stoṅ-gsum-gyi stoṅ-chen-po'i 'jig-rten-gyi khams 'di sprin[3]-gyi-dra-ba-gcig[4]-gis kun-tu-khebs-par-byed-pa daṅ / rluṅ-gi dkyil-'khor chus-'debs śes[5] bya-ba gaṅ-gis-na sreg[1]-pa'i bskal-pa'i tshe char 'bebs-par-byed-pa daṅ / rluṅ-gi dkyil-'khor lhag-par-skems śes[5] bya-ba gaṅ-gis-na / chus 'jig[6]-pa de lhag-par-skems-par-byed-pa yod-do // mo'u-dgal-gyi-bu ṅas rluṅ-gi dkyil-'khor-las brtsams[7]-te / bskal-pa'am / bskal-pa-las lhag-par chos bstan kyaṅ / de-bźin-gśegs-pas rluṅ-gi dkyil-'khor-las brtsams[7]-te / chos bstan-pa-la[8] mthar[9]-thug-pa-med-do // mo'u-dgal-gyi-bu 'di ji-sñam-du sems / sgyu-ma-mkhan bzaṅ-pos rluṅ-gi-dkyil-'khor de-dag-gi naṅ-du 'dug-par nus-sam / gsol-pa / ma lags-so // bcom-ldan-'das-kyis bka'-stsal-pa // mo'u-dgal-gyi-bu ṅa ni rluṅ-gi dkyil-'khor de-dag thams-cad[10]-kyi naṅ-du spyod-lam bźis gnas-par-byed-do // de-bźin-gśegs-pa ni bźed-na rluṅ-gi dkyil-'khor thams-cad yuṅs-'bru cig-gi naṅ-du 'jog-par mdzad / 'jug-par mdzad-la / yuṅs-'bru de yaṅ rnam-par-'jig-par mi-'gyur-źiṅ / yuṅs-'bru de'i naṅ-du rluṅ-gi dkyil-'khor de[11]-dag thams-cad-kyi bya-ba thams-cad kyaṅ[12] ñe-bar-ston-par mdzad-la / rluṅ de-dag phan-tshun thug-par yaṅ mi-'gyur / ltuṅ-bar yaṅ mi-'gyur-ro / mo'u-dgal-gyi-bu ṅa ni sgyu-ma'i chos-ñid de-lta-bu daṅ de ma-yin-pa gźan-yaṅ tshad-med-pa-daṅ-ldan-no //

10. de-nas tshe-daṅ-ldan-pa mo'u-dgal-gyi-bu-chen-po daṅ / thams-cad-daṅ-ldan-pa'i 'khor de ṅo-mtshar-du gyur-nas / bcom-ldan-'das-kyi[13] źabs-la mgo-bos phyag-'tshal-te / ṅag-mthun[14]-par tshig-tu[15] smras-pa // bcom-ldaṅ-'das bdag-cag-gis rñed-pa legs-par-rñed-do // ston-pa 'di-ltar rdzu-'phrul che-ba / 'di-ltar dbaṅ che-bar grags-pa / 'di-ltar mthu che-ba ni bdag-cag-gis[16] rñed-pa legs-par-rñed-pa[17]-lags-so bcom-ldan-'das gaṅ-dag de-bźin-gśegs-pa'i cho-'phrul 'di thos-nas mos-par-bgyid-ciṅ / mos-par-bgyis-nas kyaṅ bla-na-med-pa yaṅ-dag-par-rdzogs-pa'i byaṅ-chub-tu sems bskyed-par-bgyid-pa de-dag kyaṅ rñed-pa legs-par-rñed-pa-lags-so //

---

[1] N bsreg [2] BP *om.* bya-ba [3] B spron [4] BP cig [5] B źes [6] B 'jigs [7] B btsams [8] N las [9] BP mtha' [10] B *om.* cad [11] B 'di [12] B *om.* [13] B kyis [14] BP 'thun [15] BP du [16] B *ad.* legs-par [17] BP. *om.* pa.

11. de-nas sgyu-ma-mkhan bzaṅ-po rgyal-po'i khab-kyi groṅ-khyer chen-po ga-la-ba-der soṅ-ste / de-ñid-kyi nub-mo rgyal-po'i khab-kyi groṅ-khyer chen-po'i phyogs gaṅ-na groṅ-khyer thams-cad-kyi brtsog[1]-dgu daṅ / mi-mthun[2]-pa thams-cad 'bab-pa daṅ 'gyur-ba'i sa-phyogs der 'khor-gyi[3] khyams chen-po[4] dar-gyi lda-ldi daṅ / gdugs daṅ rgyal-mtshan daṅ / ba-dan bsgreṅ-bas brgyan-pa / gźi lag-mthil-ltar mñan-pa me-tog bkram-pa / spos bzaṅ-po mchog-gis btugs[5]-pa / steṅ-du bla-re bres-pa źig mṅon-par-sprul-te[6] / khor-gyi[7] khyams de'i naṅ-du yaṅ rin-po-che'i śiṅ-ljon-pa me-tog daṅ 'bras-bur bcas-pa / brgyad[8]-stoṅ mṅon-par-sprul-to // rin-po-che'i śiṅ[9]-ljon-pa thams-cad-kyi druṅ-du yaṅ / seṅ-ge'i khri ras-bcos-bu du-mas gyogs-pa / rin-po-che'i ba-dan thams-cad-kyis brgyan-pa mṅon-par-sprul-to // seṅ-ge'i khri'i gyas-gyon-tu[10] yaṅ rin-po-che'i śiṅ-ljon-pa me-tog daṅ / 'bras-bur[11] bcas-pa bźi-bźi mṅon-par-sprul-to // bcom-ldan-'das daṅ dge-sloṅ-gi dge-'dun-gyis yoṅs-su-loṅs-spyod-par bya-ba'i źal-zas ro-brgya-daṅ-ldan-pa yaṅ mṅon-par-sprul-to // rim-'gro-byad-pa gos dkar-po bgos-pa / rgyan thams-cad-kyis brgyan-pa lṅa-brgya yaṅ mṅon-par-sprul-to //

12. sgyu-ma-mkhan bzaṅ-pos bkod-pa de-lta-bur sprul ma-thag-tu de-nas de'i mod-la rgyal-po chen-po bźi lus chen-por sprul-nas / sgyu-ma-mkhan bzaṅ-po'i 'khor-gyi[12] khyams-kyi bkod-pa ga-la-ba-der soṅ-nas / sgyu-ma-mkhan bzaṅ-po-la 'di-skad ces smras-so // bzaṅ-po khyod-kyis de-bźin-gśegs-pa[13] saṅ[14]-gdugs-tshod-la spyan-draṅs-pa daṅ / khyod-kyis de-bźin-gśegs-pas yoṅs-su-loṅs-spyod[15]-par bya-ba'i 'khor-gyi khyams-kyi bkod-pas 'di-lta-bu 'di mṅon-par-sprul-pa ni rñed-pa legs-par-rñed-do // bzaṅ-po gźan-yaṅ kho-bo-cag kyaṅ de-bźin-gśegs-pa-la mchod-pa'i[16] las bya-ba-la / bcom-ldan-'das-kyis yoṅs-su-loṅs-spyod-pa[17] daṅ / khyod-la bstaṅ-ba'i[18] phyir 'khor-gyi[12] khyams-kyi bkod-pa 'di-lta-bu gñis-pa chuṅ-źig ston-par-byed[19]-na / kho-bo-cag-la gnaṅ-bar-gyis-śig / de-nas sgyu-ma-mkhan bzaṅ-po śin-tu-ṅo[20]-mtshar-du-gyur-nas /

---

[1] P btsog [2] BP 'thun [3] B gyis, P kyis [4] BP por [5] B gdugs [6] N to [7] BP kyi [8] BP brgya [9] B *om.* śiṅ [10] B gyags-gyogs-su [11] BP bus [12] P kyi [13] B pas [14] B *om.* saṅ [15] N spyad [16] *between* mchod *and* pa'i, P *ins.* pa bya ba'i las [17] B *om.* pa [18] BP bstod-pa'i [19] BP *ad.* pa [20] P mṅo

rgyal-po chen-po bźi-la gnaṅ-ba daṅ / de-nas rgyal-po chen-po bźis / bcom-ldan-'das-kyis yoṅs-su-loṅs-spyod[1]-par bya-ba'i 'khor-gyi[2] khyams de-lta-bu źig-mṅon-par-sprul-to //

13. de-nas yaṅ lha-rnams-kyi dbaṅ-po[3] brgya-byin lha'i bu sum-khri daṅ lhan-cig bzaṅ-po'i 'khor-gyi[2] khyams-kyi bkod-pa ga-la-ba-der soṅ-nas / sgyu-ma-mkhan bzaṅ-po-la 'di-skad ces smras-so // bzaṅ-po khyod-kyis de-bźin-gśegs-pa saṅ-gdugs-tshod-la spyan-draṅs-pa daṅ / de-bźin-gśegs-pas yoṅs-su-loṅs-spyod-pa bya-ba'i 'khor-gyi[2] khyams-kyi bkod-pa 'di-lta-bu 'di mṅon-par-sprul-pa ni rñed-pa legs-par-rñed-do // bzaṅ-po kho-bo[4]-cag kyaṅ de-bźin-gśegs-pa-la mchod-pa'i las-bya źiṅ / bcom-ldan-'das-kyis[5] yoṅs-su-loṅs-spyod[1]-pa daṅ / khyod-la bstaṅ-ba'i[6] phyir 'khor-gyi khyams-kyi bkod-pa 'di-lta-bu gñis-pa cuṅ-źig ston-par-byed-na / kho-bo-cag-la gnaṅ-bar-gyis-śig / de-nas sgyu-ma-mkhan bzaṅ-po śin-tu-ṅo-mtshar-du-gyur-nas / lha-rnams-kyi dbaṅ-po brgya-byin-la gnaṅ-ba daṅ / de-nas lha-rnams-kyi dbaṅ-po brgya-byin-gyis / bcom-ldan-'das-kyis yoṅs-su-loṅs-spyod-par bya-ba'i[7] sum-cu[8]-rtsa-gsum-pa'i lha-rnams-kyi khaṅ-bzaṅs rnam-par-rgyal-byed daṅ / yoṅs-'du-sa-brtol-bas ches khyad-par-du 'phags-pa'i 'khor-gyi[2] khyams cig[9] mṅon-par-sprul-te / 'khor-gyi[2] khyams des sgyu-ma-mkhan bzaṅ-po'i bkod-pa daṅ / rgyal-po-chen-po bźi'i bkod-pa yaṅ mog-mog-por-byas-par gyur-to //

14. de-nas sgyu-ma-mkhan bzaṅ-po 'di-sñam-du sems-te / lha'i bu 'di-lta-bu 'di-dag kyaṅ bcom-ldan-'das-la rim-gro bya-ba daṅ / mchod-pa'i las bya-ba'i phyir mṅon-par-brtson-te / lhags-pa daṅ sbyar-na / sems-can 'di ni tha-mal-pa ma-yin-pas / bdag-gis sems-can-mchog de-lta-bu-la tho-btsams[10]-par gyur-na mi-ruṅ-gis / bya-ba 'di-lta-bu 'di-dag dor gor-ma-chag sñam-mo // de-nas sgyu-ma-mkhan bzaṅ-pos[11] sprul-pa'i bya-ba de-dag 'dor-bar byed / de-dag med-par byed-de / gsaṅ-sṅags daṅ / rigs-sṅags-kyi stobs-bskyed-pa thams-cad[12]-kyis[13] med-par byed-ciṅ / mi-snaṅ-bar bya-bar brgal kyaṅ / źal-zas daṅ / rim-gro[14]-ba[15] daṅ / 'khor-gyi[2] khyams-kyi bkod-pa daṅ / seṅ-ge'i khri yaṅ de-kho-na bźin-du snaṅ-ste / gsaṅ-sṅags daṅ rigs-sṅags-kyi stobs-bskyed-pa thams-

---

[1] N spyad [2] P kyi [3] BP rgyal-po [4] P *om.* bo [5] P kyi [6] BP bstod-pa'i [7] BP ba [8] P bcu [9] N *om.* cig mṅon-par-sprul-te / khor-gyi khyams [10] N brtsams [11] NP po [12] B *om.* cad [13] B kyi [14] P 'gro [15] N *om.* ba

cad-kyis med-par-bya ma-nus-pa daṅ / de śin-tu-ṅo-mtshar-du-gyur-nas 'di-sñam-du sems-te / bdag sṅon-chad ni 'dod-na sgyu-ma ston-par yaṅ byed[1] / 'dod-na sgyu-ma-med-par yaṅ byed-na / de[2] ni de-bźin-gśegs-pa'i ched-du gnas-kyi-bkod-pa byas-pa med-par-byed ma-nus-so sñam-mo //

15. de-nas lha-rnams-kyi dbaṅ-po brgya-byin-gyis[3] sgyu-ma-mkhan bzaṅ-po'i sems-kyi rnam-par-rtog-pa de[4] sems-kyis yoṅs-su-śes-nas / sgyu-ma-mkhan bzaṅ-po-la 'di-skad ces smras-so // bzaṅ-po ji-ltar khyod-kyis de-bźin-gśegs-pa'i phyir gnas-kyi bkod-pa byas-pa[5] 'di med-par-bya ma[6]-nus-pa / de-bźin-du bzaṅ-po gaṅ-dag sems[7] de-bźin-gśegs-pa-la sems-bskyed-pa 'ga'-tsam thob-pa de-dag-gi sems-bskyed-pa de yaṅ med-par mi-'gyur-te de-dag-gi de ni yoṅs-su-mya-ṅan-las-'das-pa'i[8] bar-gyi rgyur 'gyur-ro // de-nas sgyu-ma-mkhan bzaṅ-po dga' mgu[9] yid[10]-raṅs-te rab-tu-dga'-źiṅ yid-bde-bar gyur-nas / de-ñid-kyis mtshan-mo 'das-pa daṅ bcom-ldan-'das-la gdugs-tshod-la bab-la skul-bar byed-de[11] bcom-ldan-'das gdugs-tshod-lags-pa'i dus daṅ / tshod-la bab-na de[12] gdugs-tshod-la bab-par dgoṅs-su-gsol źes gsol-to //

16. de-nas bcom-ldan-'das sṅa-dro'i dus-kyi tshe śam-thabs mnabs[13] daṅ[14] / chos-gos gsol / lhuṅ-bzed thogs-te / dge-sloṅ-gi dge-'dun-gyis yoṅs-su[15]-bskor[16]-ciṅ dge-sloṅ-gi dge-'dun-gyi daṅ-la gśegs-te / rgyal-po'i khab-kyi groṅ-khyer-chen-por gśegs-nas / sgyu-ma-mkhan bzaṅ-po'i 'khor-gyi[17] khyams ga-la-ba-der gśegs-te / gaṅ-gis ni[18] sgyu-ma-mkhan bzaṅ[19]-po yaṅ de-bźin-gśegs-pa ni bdag-gis-sprul-pa'i bkod-pa-na bźugs-so sñam-du śes[20] rgyal-po-chen-po bźi[21] yaṅ de-bźin-gśegs-pa ni bdag-cag-gis sprul-pa'i bkod-pa-na bźugs[22]-so sñam-du śes / lha-rnams-kyi dbaṅ-po brgya-byin yaṅ / de-bźin-gśegs-pa ni bdag-gis[23] sprul-pa'i bkod-pa-na bźugs[22]-so sñam-du śes-par-'gyur-ba de-lta-bu'i rdzu-'phrul mṅon-par-'du-mdzad-pa mṅon-par-'du[24]-mzad-do // rgyal-po'i khab-kyi groṅ-khyer chen-po de-na gźan mu-stegs-can daṅ / spyod-pa-pa daṅ kun-tu-rgyu daṅ / bram-ze daṅ / khyim-bdag gaṅ-dag-gis thos-pa de-dag ni ṅo-mtshar-du gyur-nas / 'khor-gyi khyams der[25] doṅ-

---

[1] P med [2] N *om.* [3] P kyis [4] BP *om.* [5] BP bya-ba [6] P mi [7] N *om.* [8] B pa [9] N dgu [10] BN yi [11] BP do [12] B da [13] B man bas, P mnams [14] BP *om.* [15] BP *om.* su [16] B bskur [17] P kyi [18] N na [19] BP *om.* bzaṅ [20] P *ad.* pa [21] B bźis [22] P bźug [23] P gi [24] N *om.* 'du [25] B de

ste / de-riṅ dge-sbyoṅ go'u-ta-ma-la tho-'tsham-pa[1] blta[2]-bar-bya'o sñam-mo // rgyal-po'i khab-kyi groṅ-khyer chen-po de-na dad-pa'i dge-sloṅ daṅ / dge-sloṅ-ma daṅ / dge-bsñen[3] daṅ / dge-bsñen[3]-ma gaṅ-dag 'khor-ba de-dag ni 'khor-gyi dkyil-'khor der doṅ-nas / de-riṅ de-bźin-gśegs-pa-la bgam-pa[4] yaṅ mñan[5]-par-bya cho-'phrul-chen-po yaṅ blta-bar-bya'o sñam-mo //

17. de-nas sgyu-ma-mkhan bzaṅ-pos ṅa-rgyal daṅ rgyags-pa daṅ / kheṅs-pa ṅes-par-bcom-nas / bcom-ldan-'das-kyi źabs-la mgo-bos[6] phyag[7]-'tshal-te / bcom-ldan-'das-la 'di-skad ces gsol-to / bcom-ldan-'das rnam-par-tho-btsam[8]-pa'i bsam-pa chen-pos de-bźin-gśegs-pa 'dir gśegs[9]-su gsol-ba gaṅ lags-pa'i noṅs-pa ᶜchags-so // bcom-ldan-'das gźan-yaṅ źal-zas sprul-pa daṅ / rim-'gro[10]-bgyid-pa sprul-pa daṅ / seṅ-ge'i khri sprul-pa daṅ 'khor-gyi khyams sprul-pa de-la bdag 'di-sñam-du sems-can-mchog de-lta-bu de-la bslus-par gyur-na / mi-ruṅ-gis[11] / bya-ba 'di ma-mchis-par-bgyi sñam-ste[12] / śin-tu-spaṅs kyaṅ ma-mchis-par ma-btub[13] gsaṅ-sṅags daṅ rigs-sṅags-kyi stobs-bskyed-pa thams-cad-kyis[14] kyaṅ-ma-mchis-par-bgyi rṅo[15]-ma-thogs[16]-nas / źal-zas daṅ rim-'gro[10] bgyid-pa daṅ / seṅ-ge'i khri daṅ 'khor-gyi khyams-kyi bkod-pa yaṅ de-kho-na bźin-du gda'o[17] / de-skad ces gsol-ba daṅ //

18. bcom-ldan-'das-kyis sgyu-ma-mkhan bzaṅ-po-la 'di-skad ces bka'-stsal-to // bzaṅ-po sems-can thams-cad-kyi ñe-bar-spyad-pa daṅ / yoṅs-su-spyad-pa yaṅ 'di-lta-ste / las-kyi sgyu-mas sprul-pa yin-no // bzaṅ-po dge-sloṅ-gi dge-'duṅ 'di yaṅ 'di-lta-ste / chos-kyi sgyu-mas sprul-pa yin-no // bzaṅ-po ṅa yaṅ 'di-lta-ste / ye-śes-kyi sgyu-mas sprul-pa yin-no // bzaṅ-po stoṅ-gsum-gyi stoṅ-chen-po'i 'jig-rten-gyi khams 'di yaṅ 'di-lta-ste // sna-tshogs mṅon-par-'grub-par byed-pa'i sgyu-mas sprul-pa yin-no // bzaṅ-po chos-thams-cad kyaṅ 'di-lta-ste / rkyen-tshogs-pa'i sgyu-mas sprul-pa yin-no // bzaṅ-po 'on-kyaṅ da[18] de'i dus-la bab-par śes-na ji-ltar sprul-pa'i bza'-ba daṅ / bca'-ba daṅ / myaṅ-ba daṅ / bldag-pa-dag khyod-kyis phul-cig / de-nas sgyu-ma-mkhan bzaṅ-pos[19] sprul-pa'i rim-'gro-ba[20] de-dag daṅ / rgyal-po chen-po bźi-dag

---

[1] N par [2] B lta [3] B bsñan, P sñen [4] BP dka'-ba [5] B mñam [6] B *om.* mgo-bos [7] P *om.* phyag [8] N brtsam [9] P gśes [10] B gro [11] B gi [12] N te [13] P btugs [14] B *ins.* ma [15] N rṅom [16] P thog [17] P gaṅ-la [18] N *om.* [19] BP po [20] B pa

daṅ / lha'i dbaṅ-po brgya-byin-daṅ bcas-pa daṅ / lhan-cig sprul-pa'i bza'-ba daṅ bca'-ba[1] daṅ / myaṅ-ba daṅ bldag-pa des bcom-ldan-'das daṅ / dge-sloṅ-gi dge-'dun yaṅ-dag-par-tshim-par byed-do //

19. de-nas de'i tshe gnas-brtan 'od-sruṅ[2] chen-pos // tshigs-su-bcad-pa 'di smras-so //

sbyin-pa 'di ni ci[3]-'dra daṅ[4]
len-par-byed-pa ci-'dra-ba
de-'dra'i chos-ñid thob-'gyur-bar[5]
yon ni rnam-par-sbyoṅ gyur-cig

20. mo'u[6]-dgal-gyi-bu-chen-pos smras-pa //

gdan ni ji-ltar bśams-pa daṅ
de-la gaṅ-dag bźugs-pa-rnams
mi-mñam-ma-mchis mtshuṅs-pa-ste
mchod-sbyin-dag-pa[7] bla-na-med

21. śā-ri'i-bus[8] smras-pa //

rim-gro-byed-pa'i sems gaṅ daṅ
len-par-byed-pa'i sems gaṅ daṅ
sbyin-par-byed-pa ji-lta-bur
yon ni myur-du sbyoṅ-bar śog[9]

22. rab-'byor-gyis[10] smras-pa //

gtoṅ-med sbyin-pa 'di btaṅ-ba[11]
len-pa-med-pa-rnams-kyis blaṅs
gaṅ-dag 'dir ni gśegs-pa-rnams
de-dag yon sbyoṅ byed-pa yin

23. kun-dga'-bos smras pa //

'di ni nam-mkha'i[12] sbyin-pa-ste
bsam-gyis-mi-khyab-rnams-kyis spyad[13]
gaṅ-dag sems-lus-grol-ba de
'jig-rten-na[14] ni[15] yon sbyoṅ mchog

---

[1] P bcas-pa [2] B sruṅs [3] N ci-źig, P 'ci [4] N *om.* [5] B bgyid-par, N 'gyur-ba [6] BP me'u [7] N dge-ba [8] P śa-ri-bus [9] P śob [10] P kyis [11] N bas [12] BP mkha' [13] B sbyad [14] B pa, N dag [15] BN na

24\. byaṅ-chub-sems-dpa' 'od-tog-gis smras-pa //
ji-lta-bur-na sgyu-ma'i mkhan
bzaṅ-pos bkod-pa sprul-byas-pa
dṅos-kun de daṅ 'dra-ba-ste
byis-pas de ni mi-rtogs-so

25\. byaṅ-chub-sems-dpa' 'od-bkod-pas smras-pa //
ji-ltar gdan daṅ ljon-śiṅ-dag
du-ma mṅon-par-sprul-byas-pa
yid-kyi sgyu-ma lta-bur stoṅ[1]
'di-la khyad-par 'ga' yaṅ med

26\. byaṅ-chub-sems-dpa' seṅ-ges[2] smras-pa //
seṅ-ge'i sgra ni ma-thos-na
wa ni nags-tshal naṅ-na sgrogs
de-yi[3] seṅ-ge'i-sgra thos-nas
phyogs-bcu-dag-tu[4] 'bros-par-'gyur

27\. de-bźin sgyu-mkhan bzaṅ-po yaṅ
de-bźin-gśegs-pas ma-mthoṅ-na
mu-stegs-naṅ-du[5] rgyal-ba-bas
bdag-ñid mchog ces sgrags-par-byed

28\. bzaṅ-po de-bźin-gśegs-pa-yi[6]
sgyu-mas sgyu-mar rtogs-byed-pa
tshad-mar-gyur-pa gsuṅs-na ni
de-la bdud-kyis gtiṅ mi[7]-dpogs

29\. byaṅ-chub-sems-dpa' seṅ-ge'i-blo-gros-kyis[8] smras-pa //
źal-zas 'di ni sprul-pa ste
bsñen-bkur-byed[9] pa'aṅ[10] sprul-pa[11] yin
spyod-par-byed pa'aṅ sprul-pa-ste
sbyin-pa dge-ba bla-na-med

30\. byaṅ-chub-sems-dpa' byams-pas smras-pa //
me ni mar daṅ til-mar-gyis
phyi[12]-phyir źiṅ ni rab-tu mched[13]
de-bźin bzaṅ-po'i sgyu-ma-yis
saṅs-rgyas-sgyu-ma ṅes-par-bstan

---

[1] BP ston [2] P *ad.* sgras [3] BP de'i [4] P du [5] N na [6] B yis [7] B mig [8] P gyis [9] B *om.* byed [10] BP 'am [11] P *om* ad. [12] BP phyir [13] B rab-mched-pa, N mche

31. 'jam-dpal-gźon-nur-gyur-pas smras-pa //
ji-ltar 'di ni[1] sṅon gnas-pa
thams-cad byed-pa-med-pa ltar
de-bźin chos-rnams thams-cad ni
sṅon-gyi mtha'-nas rtag-tu mñam

32. de-nas bcom-ldan-'das-kyis sgyu-ma-mkhan bzaṅ-po śin-tu-gdul-ba'i dbaṅ-du mdzad-nas / khyim-bdag gcig[2] sprul-te / 'khor-gyi[3] khyams de'i naṅ-du źugs-nas / sgyu-ma-mkhan bzaṅ-po-la 'di-skad ces smras-so // bzaṅ-po ci-byed / smras-pa // dge-sbyoṅ go'u-ta-ma 'di gdugs-tshod gsol-bar byed-do // des smras-pa // bzaṅ-po thoṅ[4] de-skad ma-zer // de-bźin-gśegs-pa[5] de ni dge-sloṅ-gi dge-'dun daṅ thabs-gcig[2]-tu / rgyal-po[6] ma-skyes-dgra'i khab-na gdugs-tshod-gsol-źiṅ bźugs-so // sgyu-ma-mkhan bzaṅ-pos kyaṅ saṅs-rgyas-kyi mthus de-bźin-gśegs-pa dge-sloṅ-gi dge-'dun daṅ thabs-gcig[2]-tu rgyal-po ma-skyes-dgra'i khab-ba gdugs-tshod gsol-bar mthoṅ-ṅo // de-nas yaṅ bcom-ldan-'das-kyis khyim-bdag gñis-pa źig mṅon-par-sprul-nas de naṅ-du źugs-te / sgyu-ma-mkhan bzaṅ-po-la 'di-skad ces smras-so // bzaṅ-po ci-byed / smras-pa[7] // dge-sbyoṅ go'u-ta-ma 'di gdugs-tshod gsol-bar byed-do[8] // des smras-pa // bzaṅ-po[9] thoṅ de-skad[10] ma-zer // de-bźin-gśegs-pa de ni dge-sloṅ-gi dge-'dun daṅ thabs-gcig[2]-tu kun-tu-rgyu'i sraṅ-na bsod-sñoms-kyi phyir rgyu-źiṅ[11] bźugs-so // sgyu-ma-mkhan bzaṅ-pos kyaṅ saṅs-rgyas-kyi mthus de-bzin-gśegs-pa dge-sloṅ-gi dge-'dun daṅ thabs-gcig[2]-tu kun-tu-rgyu'i sraṅ-na bsod-sñoms-kyi phyir rgyu-bar[12] mthoṅ-ṅo // de-nas bcom-ldan-'das-kyis khyim-bdag gźan-źig sprul-te / de naṅ-du źugs-nas sgyu-ma-mkhan bzaṅ-po-la[13] 'di-skad ces smras-so // bzaṅ-po ci-byed / smras-pa // de-bźin-gśegs-pa 'di gdugs-tshod gsol-bar byed-do // des smras-pa // bzaṅ-po thoṅ[4] de-skad ma-zer / de-bźin-gśegs-pa de ni 'tsho-byed-kyi skyed[14]-mos-tshal-na 'khor bźi-la chos ston-ciṅ[15] bźugs-so // sgyu-ma-mkhan bzaṅ-pos kyaṅ saṅs-rgyas-kyi mthus de-bźin-gśegs-pa 'tsho-byed-kyi skyed[14]-mos[16]-tshal-na[17] 'khor bźi-la chos-ston-par mthoṅ-ṅo // de-nas

---

[1] B na [2] BP cig [3] P kyi [4] B thoṅs [5] B *om.* pa [6] B *om. the words from* rgyal-po *down to* thabs-cig, P rgyal-po'i [7] P smras-so [8] P de [9] P *om.* bzaṅ-po [10] N sgad [11] N *om.* rgyu-źiṅ [12] N ba [13] P *om.* la [14] BN bskyed [15] BP źiṅ [16] P mo [17] P ni

lha-rnams-kyi dbaṅ-po brgya-byin sgyu-ma-mkhan bzaṅ-po ga-la-ba-der soṅ-ste phyin-nas / sgyu-ma-mkhan bzaṅ-po-la 'di-skad ces smras-so // bzaṅ-po ci-byed / smras-pa // dge-sbyoṅ go'u-ta-ma 'di gdugs-tshod gsol-bar byed-do // des smras-pa // bzaṅ-po thoṅ[1] de-skad ma-zer // de-bźin-gśegs-pa de ni sum-cu-rtsa-gsum-pa'i gnas-na / śiṅ yoṅs-'du'i druṅ-na / sum-cu-rtsa-gsum-pa'i lha-rnams-la chos ston-ciṅ bźugs[2]-so // bzaṅ-pos kyaṅ de-bźin-gśegs-pa sum-cu-rtsa-gsum-pa'i gnas-na śiṅ yoṅs-'du'i druṅ-na chos ston-par mthoṅ-ṅo //

33. de-nas yaṅ sgyu-ma-mkhan bzaṅ-pos śiṅ-ljon-pa sprul-pa ji-sñed-pa[3] de thams-cad-kyi lo-ma thams-cad daṅ / me-tog thams-cad-la de-bźin-gśegs-pa'i sku mtshan-gyis brgyan-pa / dge-sloṅ-gi dge-'dun-gyis yoṅs-su-bskor-ba mthoṅ-ṅo // sgyu-ma-mkhan bzaṅ-pos seṅ-ge'i khri sprul-pa gaṅ-dag yin-pa daṅ / rgyal-po chen-po bźis seṅ-ge'i khri sprul-pa gaṅ-dag yin-pa de-dag[4] thams-cad-la yaṅ de-bźin-gśegs-pa'i sku mtshan-gyis[5] brgyan-pa dge-sloṅ-gi dge-'dun-gyis yoṅs-su-bskor-ba mthoṅ-ṅo // rgyal-po'i[6] khab-kyi groṅ-khyer chen-po-na rtsig-pa'am / khyim-mam / khaṅ-bzaṅs-sam / sraṅ-ṅam / lam-po-che ji-sñed yod-pa de-dag thams-cad-na yaṅ de-bźin-gśegs-pa'i sku mtshan-gyis brgyan-pa mthoṅ-ṅo // de-bźin-gśegs-pa dgra-bcom-pa yaṅ-dag-par-rdzogs-pa'i saṅs-rgyas de-dag thams-cad[7]-kyi spyan-sṅar[8] yaṅ sgyu-ma-mkhan bzaṅ-po bdag-ñid phyag-'tshal-nas ñes-pa[9] 'chags-par mthoṅ-źiṅ de-na sgyu-ma-mkhan bzaṅ-po'i[10] mig-lam-na gaṅ cuṅ[11]-zad ci snaṅ-ba thams-cad de-bźin-gśegs-pa ma-gtogs-pa gźan cuṅ-zad kyaṅ ma-mthoṅ-nas / de tshim-źiṅ mgu-la yid[12]-raṅs-te / rab-tu[13]-dga'-źin dga'-ba daṅ yid-bde-bar gyur-to // de dga'-ba daṅ yid-bde-ba de-ñid-kyis dad-pa-rjes-su-dran-pa'i tiṅ-ṅe-'dzin thob-bo // de tiṅ-ṅe-'dzin de-las laṅs ma-thag-tu / thal-mo sbyar-te / bcom-ldan-'das-kyi spyan-sṅar 'dug-nas tshigs-su-bcad-pa 'di-dag gsol-to //

34. bźed-na[14] brgya-phrag stoṅ-las lhag gyur-ciṅ[15]
dper-na gaṅ-ga'i kluṅ-gi bye sñed-kyi
saṅs-rgyas maṅ-po sprul-par mdzad-pa-yi
de-bźin-gśegs-kyi rdzu-'phrul de-la mos

---

[1] B thoṅs [2] BP gźugs [3] N *om.* pa [4] BP *om.* dag [5] P kyis [6] P po [7] B *om.* cad [8] N sṅa-na [9] B *om.* pa [10] N po [11] BP chuṅ [12] BN yi [13] BP du [14] B pa [15] BP cig

35. bdag-gis sṅon bslabs[1] sgyu-ma'i sa ma-lags
'dzam-bu'i gliṅ-na bdag-dra-med sñam-na
de-riṅ rgyal-ba'i rdzu-'phrul 'di mthoṅ-nas
'di-yi graṅs daṅ char[2] yaṅ ma-phod[3]-do

36. bdag-gi śa-yi[4] mig[5]-gis gaṅ mthoṅ-ba
thams-cad rgyal-ba'i mtshan-gyis[6] brgyan-pa'i sku
chos-kyi rgyal-po-la ni 'di-dag źus
rgyal-ba yaṅ-dag gaṅ lags bka'-stsol-cig

37. gaṅ-źig mchod-na legs-par-mchod-pa lags
gaṅ-la 'bras-bu chen-por 'gyur-ba lags
gaṅ-gi byaṅ-chub mthun[7]-par gzuṅ-ba 'di
kun-tu-spyan-gyis bdag-la bka'-stsol-cig

38. de-riṅ 'jig-rten-mgon[8]-la bgam-bgyis-pa'i
noṅs-pa gaṅ lags deṅ[9] 'dir kun-tu-'chags
gaṅ-dag sems-can-mchog-la gus mi-gnas
sems-can de-dag rgyal-ba'i bde-las[10] ñams

39. bdag-la lha daṅ brgya-byin tshaṅs-pa daṅ
'khor-'dus-gyur-pa 'di-dag kun gson-cig
sems-can thams-cad rab-tu-dgrol slad-du
byaṅ-chub-sems ni bdag-gis[11] bskyed-par-bgyi

40. bdag-gis sems-can thams-cad mgron[12]-du gñer
bdud-rtsi bde-bas yaṅ-dag-tshim-par-bgyi
gñid-kyis rab-log sems-can śes-rab-kyi[13]
mthu daṅ sgrub-pas rnam-par-sad-par-gyis[14]

41. rnam-par-'phrul-ba 'di-'dra mthoṅ-gyur-ciṅ[15]
bde-bar-gśegs bka' yid-'oṅ ye-śes daṅ
chags-pa med-pa'i spyod-mchog thos-nas ni
su-źig dag-pa'i rgyu sems-bskyed[16] mi-bgyi[17]

42. byaṅ-chub-sems-mkhas ji-ltar spyod-pa-yi
byaṅ-chub-lam ni bdag-la bśad-du-gsol
gaṅ-la ñan-thos-rnams-kyis mi-dpogs-pa'i
de-dag-rnams-kyi spyod-pa ji-lta-bu

---

[1] N bslobs [2] BP cha [3] BN spyod [4] BP śa'i [5] P myig [6] P kyis [7] BP 'thun [8] B mgo [9] BP der [10] BP la [11] B rab-tu *instead of* bdag-gis [12] BP 'gron [13] N śes-par-bgyi [14] N bgyi [15] N cig [16] BP skyed [17] BP bgyid

43. cho-ga-spyod-pa'i yon-tan ji-lta-bu
mñan-par-'dod-la gus-pa ji-lta-bu
des-pa-rnams-kyi spyod-pa[1] ci-'dra-ba[2]
bdag-la the-tshom[3]-ma-mchis de-bźin gsuṅs

44. ji-ltar thos-pa-tshol-la goms-pa lags
thos-pa sñiṅ-por-bgyid-pa'i daṅ-po gaṅ
gźan-la gsal-bar ston-pa ji-lta-bu
srog-chags thams-cad ji-ltar chos-la dad

45. ji-ltar 'di-dag śes-kyi khe mi-tshol
zaṅ-ziṅ-med-pa'i sems-la ji-ltar gnas
byas-pa[4]-śes-śiṅ rab-tu[5]-phan-'dogs daṅ
sems-can mi-phyed gnas-par ji-ltar 'gyur

46. grogs-po gaṅ-dag bsten-bgyi ji-lta-bu
sdig-pa'i grogs-rnams ji-ltar rnam-par-spoṅ
ji-ltar saṅs-rgyas-rnams daṅ phrad-par-'gyur
de-dag mthoṅ-nas ji-ltar mchod-pa bgyi

47. ji-ltar bslab-pa dag-la gus-pa lags
de-yi bslab-pa'i[6] bca'-ba gaṅ-źig lags
tshul-khrims ji-ltar rnam-par-dag-par 'gyur
tiṅ-'dzin rnam-par-dag-pa[7] ji-ltar 'thob[8]

48. ji-ltar tshul-bźin rab-tu[9]-sbyor-ba lags
tshul-bźin ma-lags ji-ltar spoṅ-ba lags
ji-ltar śin-tu-ṅes-par bsam[10]-yid daṅ
ñon-moṅs bdud-kyi 'chiṅ[11]-bas mi-thub lags

49. ji-ltar dad[12]-ldan don ni sems bgyid-ciṅ
sems-kyis sems-can-rnams ni mi-gtoṅ lags
ji-ltar sems-can yoṅs-su-smin-bgyid-ciṅ
nor-mchog 'dzin-pa-med-la dpa'-ba lags

50. ji-ltar sems-can spyod-la 'jug-pa daṅ
thabs[13] daṅ byams-pa sñiṅ-rjes gnas-pa lags
mṅon-par-śes-pa ji-ltar yoṅs-rdzogs-'gyur
dran daṅ blo-gros gaṅ-gis rnam-dag-ciṅ

---

[1] N spyod-lam [2] B 'dra-ci-ba [3] B mtsho [4] P byas-pa-pa
[5] BP du [6] BP pa [7] B par [8] N 'thobs [9] BP du [10] N bsams
[11] N bciṅ [12] P daṅ [13] BNP thams

51. so-so-yaṅ-dag-rig gzuṅs bzod-par 'gyur
smon-lam rnam-dag spyod-las mi-ldog-ciṅ
zab-mo-śes-ldan don-dam-mkhas-pa lags
smon-lam thams-cad ji-ltar 'grub-par 'gyur

52. ji-ltar de-dag pha-rol-phyin 'phags-śiṅ
de-bźin byaṅ-chub rjes-su-mthun[1]-par 'gyur
byaṅ-chub-sems-dpa'i spyod-pa kun-śes-śiṅ
byaṅ-chub-phyir ni spyod-pa mi-ldog-pa

53. kun-mkhyen legs-par-don-bsam[2] śes-rab-mtsho
ye-śes 'byuṅ-gnas 'di ni bdag-la gsuṅs
bcom-ldan phan-yon bdag-la bstan-du gsol
bdag-gis nan-tan sñiṅ-por bgyi-bar 'tshal

54. de-nas bcom-ldan-'das-kyis sgyu-ma-mkhan bzaṅ-po-la /
slar tshigs-su-bcad de bka'-stsal-pa //

chos kun sprul-par gaṅ-gis śes-pa de
saṅs-rgyas bye-ba phrag stoṅ sprul-par byed
sprul-pa de-dag źiṅ-rnams bye-bar 'gro
de-dag soṅ-nas sems-can bye-ba 'grol[3]

55. ji-ltar bzaṅ-po khyod-kyis gzugs-med-las
sna-tshogs mtha'-yas gzugs ni ston-byed-ci
de-dag skye-ba-med-ciṅ 'gag-med-la
'gro-med 'oṅ-med gnas-pa-med-pa ltar

56. bzaṅ-po skyes-bu-khyu-mchog rgyal-ba-yis
phuṅ-po dge-'dun-tshogs-bcas sprul de-'dra
de daṅ ye-śes-med-par mi-'gyur-te
saṅs-rgyas bsam-yas-rnams-kyi rdzu-'phrul yin

57. ji-ltar sgyu-mas rmoṅs-byas skye-bo ni
sems-pa yod min de-bzin ṅa-rgyal-med
'di-la 'grub-pa-med-ciṅ rjoṅ[4] yod min
phyin-ci-log-gi sems-kyis mthoṅ-ba ltar

58. de-bzin saṅs-rgyas gzugs-med kha-dog daṅ
de-la[5] dbyibs-med[6] spyod-daṅ[7]-spyod-lam-med
'jig-tshogs lta-ba kun-nas-bslaṅ ma-yin
saṅs-rgyas saṅs-rgyas sñam-du 'du-śes-med

---

[1] BP 'thun [2] N bsams [3] N 'grel [4] N rjas [5] N *om.* de la
[6] N min [7] N pa ston yaṅ

59. saṅs-rgyas gzugs-su mi-lta mtshan daṅ ni
na-tshod rigs-su ma-yin sgra daṅ ni
'chad[1]-par-'gyur-ba ma-yin sems daṅ ni
rnam-śes yid-kyis rab-tu-phye ma-yin

60. chos-ñid gaṅ yin saṅs-rgyas bcom-ldan-'das
dus-gsum-stoṅ-źiṅ mtshan yaṅ ma-skyes-pa
rtag-tu sgyu-ma'i raṅ-bźin rnam-par-grol
de-la chos-su[2] bgraṅ-bar[3] rab-tu-phye-ba-med

61. saṅs-rgyas 'byuṅ gaṅ chos-ñid[4] 'byuṅ-ba-med
de-la phuṅ-po yod-min khams mi-'byuṅ
chos de gnas-pa mi-gyo rten[5]-pa-med
de-ni mig lṅa'i gnas kyaṅ ma-yin-no

62. gaṅ-źig bdag-gis saṅs-rgyas blta sñam-sems
des ni gźan-yaṅ saṅs-rgyas mthoṅ mi-'gyur
'dren-pa mthoṅ-ba-med-pa mthoṅ-ba-ste
dper-na nam-mkha'-la ni bya rjes bźin

63. bzaṅ-po gaṅ khyod cuṅ[6]-zad saṅs-rgyas blta[7]
de kun don-cig yin-par śes-par-gyis
ṅa daṅ gźan gaṅ yin-pa de kun mtshuṅs
bar-snaṅ mthoṅ daṅ 'dra-bar mñam-pa yin

64. de-dag tiṅ-'dzin mñam-źiṅ śes-rab-mñam
de-dag rnam-par-grol-bar mñam-pa yin
rnam-grol ye-śes mthoṅ daṅ[8] stobs daṅ ni
rgyal-ba'i yon-tan kun-gyis[9] mñam-pa yin

65. de-dag stoṅ-don go-'phaṅ gnas-par mñam
thams-cad chags-pa[10]-med-pa'i chos-ñid gnas
kun kyaṅ sgyu-ma'i raṅ-bźin rnam-par-grol
de-dag 'byuṅ-ba-med-par 'byuṅ-ba yin

66. bzaṅ-po rgyal-ba gcig[11]-la mchod-byed-na
phyogs-bcu'i saṅs-rgyas-la ni mchod-'gyur-te
'di-ltar de-dag ṅa-yi chos-dbyiṅs daṅ
tha-dad bya-ba nam-yaṅ yod ma-yin

---

[1] B 'chaṅ [2] N *om.* chos-su [3] N bas [4] BP ñis [5] P rton
[6] BP chuṅ [7] BP lta [8] B *om.* daṅ [19] P kyis [0] B *om.* pa
[11] BP cig

67. de-dag thams-cad yon bźes sbyoṅ-bar mdzad
kun-la phul-ba'aṅ 'bras-bu che-bar 'gyur
de kun chos-ñid dag-pa mñam-pa brñes
saṅs-rgyas-rnams-la tha-dad bya-ba'aṅ med

68. rgyal-ba yaṅ-dag gaṅ yin bśad-bya-yin[1]
rtse-gcig[2]-sems daṅ dran-pa[3]-ñer-bźag-ciṅ
chos tshul rtogs-la rnam[4]-par-lta-bas de
legs-par-ṅes[5]-pa[6] sems-kyis[7] ṅa-la ñon

69. bzaṅ-po de kun ma-skyes yaṅ-dag-min
phyin-ci-log-gis de kun mthoṅ-bar zad
gal-te dṅos-po'i ṅo-bo yaṅ-dag-na
dṅos-po thams-cad-du ni zad mi-'gyur

70. de-phyir śin-tu-ma-skyes yaṅ-dag-min
de-dag skye-med zad-la gnas-pa-med
des-na bltar-med ṅo-bo de-dag snaṅ
rnam-par-bltas-na gnas-pa yod ma-yin

71. ji-ltar bzaṅ-pos rgyal-ba mthoṅ-ba daṅ
ji-ltar phyogs-su mṅon-par-sprul mthoṅ-ba
gaṅ gźan phuṅ-po rgya[8]-chen rten stobs daṅ
phuṅ-po lṅa-po[9]'an de daṅ 'dra-bar ltos

72. chos-rnams thams-cad raṅ-bźin-med-pa-ste
sems-can daṅ ni saṅs-rgyas-mtshan-ñid-med
mtshan-ñid-med-la mtshan-du 'dod-pa de
saṅs-rgyas las-ni śin-tu-riṅ-bar-'gyur

73. chos yod ma-yin kun-tu-rtogs-pas bslaṅ
dṅos-po-med-par yaṅ ni brten[10]-nas-śes
byed-pa-med-ciṅ byed-pa-po-las-'das
miṅ-du 'dzin-pas stoṅ-par[11] rab-tu-ston[12]

74. gaṅ-gis[13] rgyu daṅ byed-pa[14]-rkyen min śes
des ni chags-bral-gyur-pa'i chos kyaṅ śes
'dod-chags-bral-ba'i chos-ni śes-gyur-na
des ni rnam-dag mig-gis saṅs-rgyas mthoṅ

---

[1] BP yis [2] P cig [3] P 'dren [4] B rnams [5] N ṅas [6] N *om.* pa *and ad.* bsams, P *ad.* bsams [7] P bgyis [8] N rgyal [9] N ba [10] N brtan [11] N pa [12] P bston [13] BP źig [14] N po

75. yaṅ de'i tshe tshigs-su bcad-pa-dag brjod de bstan-pana / sgyu-ma-mkhan-bzaṅ-po chos-la ṅes-par-rtog-pa daṅ / mthun[1]-pa'i bzod-pa chuṅ-du skyes-so // srog-chags lṅa-stoṅ ni bla-na-med-pa yaṅ-dag-par-rdzogs-pa'i byaṅ-chub-kyi[2] sems sṅon ma-bskyed[3]-pa skyes-so // byaṅ-chub-sems-dpa' ñis-brgya ni mi-skye-ba'i chos-la bzod-pa thob-par gyur-to // de-nas yaṅ[4] bcom-ldan-'das-kyis[5] źal-zas sprul-pa de-dag[6] gsol-nas / sgyu-ma-mkhan bzaṅ-po'i yon yoṅs-su-sbyaṅ-bar[7] bya-ba'i[8] phyir de'i tshe tshigs-su-bcad-pa 'di-dag[9] bka'-stsal-to //

76. gaṅ-gis sbyin daṅ[10] gaṅ-la sbyin
sbyin-pa ji[11]-ltar mi-rtog-pa
sbyin-pa mñam-pa de-ñid ni
bzaṅ-po-la ni yoṅs-rdzogs-śig

77. de-nas bcom-ldan-'das-la tshe-daṅ-ldan-pa kun-dga'-bos 'di-skad ces gsol-to // bcom-ldan-'das 'khor-gyi[12] khyams 'di rgyan-gyis brgyan bźin-du dguṅ bdun-du gnas-śiṅ / mi-gda'-bar mi-'gyur-bar byin-gyis brlab-du gsol // de-skad ces gsol-pa daṅ / bcom-ldan-'das-kyis 'khor-gyi[13] khyams de ji[14]-ltar rgyan-gyis[15] brgyan bźin-du źag bdun-du gnas-śiṅ mi-snaṅ-bar mi-'gyur-bar byin-gyis brlab-pa mdzad-do // de-nas bcom-ldan-'das dge-sloṅ-gi dge-'dun daṅ bcas-te / gdan[16]-las bźeṅs-nas gśegs-so //

78. de-nas yaṅ bcom-ldan-'das naṅ-du yaṅ-dag-'jog-las[17] bźeṅs-nas / chos-bstan-pa'i phyir bźugs-so // dge-sloṅ de-dag daṅ / byaṅ-chub-sems-dpa' de-dag daṅ / lha daṅ / klu daṅ / gnod-sbyin daṅ / dri-za de-dag kyaṅ / chos mñan-pa'i phyir bcom-ldan-'das-kyi thad-du doṅ-ṅo // de-nas sgyu-ma-mkhan bzaṅ-po yaṅ bcom-ldan-'das ga-la-ba-der soṅ-ste phyin-nas / bcom-ldan-'das-kyi źabs-la mgo-bos phyag-'tshal-te / bcom-ldan-'das-la lan-gsum bskor-ba byas-nas / gus-pa daṅ bcas źe-sa daṅ bcas-par thal-mo sbyar-te phyogs-gcig-tu 'dug-go / phyogs-gcig-tu dug-nas kyaṅ / bcom-ldan-'das-la sgyu-ma-mkhan bzaṅ-pos 'di-skad-ces gsol-to // bcom-ldan-'das byaṅ-chub-sems-dpa' lam gaṅ-la źugs-na / byaṅ-chub-kyi sñiṅ-por mchis-par 'gyur-ba'i byaṅ-chub-sems-dpa'-rnams-kyi lam bśad-du gsol // de-skad ces gsol-ba daṅ / bcom-ldan-'das-kyis

---

[1] BP 'thun [2] B gyi [3] P skyed [4] BP *om.* [5] P kyi [6] BP *om.* [7] N ba'i [8] N *om.* bya-ba'i [9] N *om.* dag. [10] BP pa [11] BP ci [12] P kyi [13] P *om.* gyi [14] N *om.* [15] P kyis [16] N stan [17] B las las

sgyu-ma-mkhan bzaṅ-po-la 'di-skad ces bka'-stsal-to // bzaṅ-po de'i[1] phyir legs-par-rab-tu[2]-ñon-la[3] yid-la zuṅ[4]-śig daṅ ṅas bśad-do // sgyu-ma-mkhan bzaṅ-pos bcom-ldan-'das-la legs-so // źes gsol-to[5] / bcom-ldan-'das-la ñan-pa daṅ / bcom-ldan-'das-kyis de-la 'di-skad ces bka'-stsal-to //

79. bzaṅ-po bźi-po 'di-dag ni byaṅ-chub-sems-dpa' lam gaṅ-la źugs-na byaṅ-chub-kyi sñiṅ-por 'gro-bar-'gyur-ba'i byaṅ-chub-sems-dpa'-rnams-kyi lam yin-te / bźi gaṅ źe-na / thams-cad mkhyen-pa-ñid-kyi sems mi-'dor-ba daṅ / sem-can yoṅs-su-mi-gtoṅ-ba daṅ / dge-ba'i rtsa-ba thams-cad tshol-ba-la[6] ṅoms-mi-śes-pa-ñid daṅ / dam-pa'i chos yoṅs-su-bsruṅ-ba'i phyir brtson-'grus rtsom-pa-ste / bzaṅ-po[7] bźi-po de-dag ni byaṅ-chub-sems-dpa' lam gaṅ-la źugs-na byaṅ-chub-kyi sñiṅ-por 'gro-bar 'gyur-ba'i byaṅ-chub-sems-dpa'-rnams-kyi lam yin-no //

80. bzaṅ-po bźi-po 'di-dag ni byaṅ-chub-sems-dpa'-rnams-kyi spyod-pa yoṅs-su-dag-pa yin-te / bźi gaṅ źe-na / sdom gsum yoṅs-su-dag-pa daṅ / gnas yoṅs-su-dag-pa daṅ / śes-pa yoṅs-su-dag-pa daṅ / skye-ba yoṅ-su-dag-pa-ste / bźi-po de-dag yin-no //

81. bzaṅ-po bźi-po 'di-dag ni gaṅ-la ñan-thos daṅ / raṅ-saṅs-rgyas thams-cad-kyis gtiṅ-mi-dpogs-pa'i byaṅ-chub-sems-dpa'i[8] chos yin-te / bźi gaṅ źe-na / bsam[9]-gtan zlog[10]-pa daṅ / sems-kyis rnam-par-'byed-pa daṅ / sems-can-rnams-la sñiṅ-rje-che-ba daṅ / spobs-pa daṅ skad-sna-tshogs-pa-ñid-de / bźi-po de-dag yin-no //

82. bzaṅ-po bźi-po 'di-dag ni byaṅ-chub-sems-dpa'-rnams-kyi 'phags-pa'i spyod-pa yin-te / bźi gaṅ źe-na / dgon[11]-pa-na gnas-pa daṅ / 'du-'dzi-la mi-dga'-ba daṅ / de-na gnas-na sems-can-rnams-la byams-pa daṅ / 'du-byed-rnams gaṅ-nas kyaṅ mi-'on gaṅ-du yaṅ mi-'gro-bar śes-pa-ste / bźi-po de-dag yin-no //

83. bzaṅ-po byaṅ-chub-sems-dpa' chos-bźi-daṅ-ldan-na sri-źu-che-źiṅ gus-pa-la gnas-pa źes brjod-par-bya-ste / bźi gaṅ źe-na / byaṅ-chub-sems-dpa' lus-daṅ-srog-la mi-lta-ba daṅ / sems rtag-tu dga'-ba daṅ / ṅa-rgyal daṅ dregs[12]-pa spoṅ-ba daṅ / ji-skad smras-pa de-bźin-du sgrub-pa-ste / bźi-po de-dag yin-no //

---

[1] P di'i [2] N *om.* rab-tu [3] B *om.* ñon-la [4] B zuṅs [5] P te [6] N *om.* tshol-ba-la [7] B *om. the end of this §, the §§ 80—88 and the beginning of § 89* [8] P dpa'-rnams-kyi [9] P bsams [10] N bzlog [11] P mgon [12] N grags

84. bzaṅ-po b. ch. s. dp. chos-bźi-daṅ-ldan-na spyod-lam phun-sum-tshogs-pa yin-te / bź. g. ź. na / dus-śes-pa daṅ / tshod-śes-pa daṅ / rab-tu-dben-pa daṅ / yaṅ-dag-pa-ñid-d^ ' bźi-po de-dag yin-no //

85. bzaṅ-po b. ch. s. dp. ch. bź. d. ld. na the-tshom-med-pa yin-te / bź. g. ź. n. / 'gyod-pa kun-nas ldaṅ-ba rnam-par-gnon-pa daṅ / mkhas-pa daṅ śes-rab-chen-po-la bsñen-bkur byed-pa daṅ / thos-pa'i don sems-pa daṅ / gźan-gyi ṅes-pa mi gleṅ-źiṅ gleṅ-ba gaṅ yin-pa yaṅ byams-pas gleṅ-gi skyon [1] gtsir [2]-byed-pas ma-yin-pa-ste / bźi-po de-dag yin-no //

86. bzaṅ-po b. ch. s. dp. phan-yon bźi-po 'di-dag mthoṅ-na thos-pa tshol-bar-byed-de / bź. g. ź. n. / bdag daṅ gźaṅ-gyi śes-rab sbyoṅ-ba daṅ / phyogs-bźi-nas lhags-pa-rnams-kyi the-tshom gcod-pa daṅ / dam-pa'i chos 'dzin-pa daṅ / saṅs-rgyas-kyis bsṅags-pa zad-mi-śes-pa-ste / bźi-po de-dag yin-no //

87. bzaṅ-po bźi-po 'di-dag [3] ni b. ch. s. dp.-rnams-kyi maṅ-du-thos-pa'i sñiṅ-po yin-no // bź. g. ź. n. / thos-nas chos bye-brag-tu śes-pa 'di ni 'di'i sñiṅ-po yin-no / thos-nas bya-ba-ma-yin-pa mi-byed-pa 'di ni 'di'i sñiṅ-po yin-no / thos-nas gźan-la ston-par-byed-pa 'di ni 'di'i sñiṅ-po yin-no / thos-nas don de-ñid rnam-par-grol-ba 'di-lta-ste / saṅs-rgyas bcom-ldan-'das-rnams-kyi byaṅ-chub-la gtod-par-byed-pa 'di ni 'di'i sñiṅ-po yin-te [4] / bźi-po de-dag yin-no [5] //

88. bzaṅ-po bźi-po 'di-dag ni b. ch. s. dpa' chos ston-par-byed-pa'i phan-yon yin-te / bź. g. ź. n. / las byas-nas [6] zas-la yoṅs-su-spyod-pa daṅ / chos-gos-daṅ / bsod-sñoms daṅ / mal-cha daṅ / stan daṅ / nad-gsos daṅ / sman-zoṅ-rnams rñed-pa daṅ / gźan-gyi phyogs mthu chuṅ-bar-byed-pa daṅ / chos 'dod-pa'i lha-rnams phyi-bźin-'braṅ-źiṅ de-dag-gis bsruṅs-pas bdud-kyis glags mi-rñed-pa-ste / bzaṅ-po bź. p. d. d. n. b. ch. s. dp. ch. st. p. b. p. phan-yon yin-no //

89. bzaṅ-po byaṅ-chub-sems-dpa' chos-bźi-daṅ-ldan-na gźan-dag-la chos ston-par-byed-ciṅ 'di'i tshig-gi [7] lam gzuṅ-bar 'os-par yaṅ 'gyur-te / bź. g. ź. n. / 'dod-pa-chuṅ-ba daṅ / chog-śes-pa daṅ / ṅaṅ-tshul-bzaṅ-źiṅ mñen [8]-pa daṅ / bdag-ñid-kyis [9] chos [10] sgrub [11]-pa-ste / bźi-po de-dag yin-no //

---

[1] P spyod [2] N gcir, P btsor [3] P *om.* dag [4] P de [5] P *om.* bźi-po de-dag-yin-no [6] P *ad.* kyaṅ [7] N *om.* [8] P mñin [9] BP kyi
[10] *Here ends the gap of* B [11] N grub

90. bzaṅ-po b. ch. s. dp. ch. bź. d. ld. n. śes-kyi khe-las 'byol-źiṅ zaṅ-ziṅ-med-par chos ston-pa[1] yin-te / bź. g. ź. n. / 'khor-ba-la 'jigs-pa skrod[2]-pa daṅ / 'jig-rten-gyi zaṅ-ziṅ daṅ 'du-'dzi[3] don-du mi-gñer-ba daṅ / pha-rol rjes-su-sruṅ-ba daṅ / 'phags-pa'i rigs-la gnas-pa-ste / bźi-po de-dag yin-no //

91. bzaṅ-po b. ch. s. dp. ch. bź. d. ld. n. / byas-pa-gzo[4]-ba daṅ / byas-pa-tshor-ba daṅ[5] / byas-pa-la lan-du phan-'dogs-pa yin-te / bź. g. ź. n. / gźan byaṅ-chub yaṅ-dag-par len-du[6]-'jug-pa daṅ / las byas-pa chud-mi-gzon[7]-pa daṅ / bdag-ñid-la byams-pa ltar gźan-la yaṅ byams-pa daṅ / skyes-bu-dam-pa'i rtsal[8] don-du gñer-ba-ste / bźi-po de-dag yin-no //

92. bzaṅ-po[9] b. ch. s. dp. ch. bź. d. ld. n. / sems-can-rnams-la mdza'-bśes mi-phyed-par 'gyur-te / bź. g. ź. n. / bzod-pa'i stobs-kyis[10] go bgos-pa daṅ / lan-du phan[11]-'dogs-par chuṅ[12]-zad kyaṅ re-ba-med-pa daṅ / sñiṅ-rje chen-po mi-'dor-ba daṅ / log-par-źugs-pa-rnams mi-spoṅ-ba-ste / b. ch. s. dp. ch. bźi-po-de-dag d.-ld.-na sems-can-rnams-la mdza'-bśes mi-phyed-par 'gyur-ro //

93. bzaṅ-po bźi-po[13] 'di-dag ni b. ch. s. dpas[14] bsten[15]-par bya-ba'i grogs-po yin-te / bź. g. ź. n. / sbyor-ba-phun-sum-tshogs-pa daṅ / bsam-pa-phun-sum-tshogs-pa daṅ / spyod-pa-phun-sum-tshogs-pa daṅ / gaṅ-dag 'di'i byaṅ-chub ñe-bar-ston[16]-par-byed-pa-ste / bźi-po de-dag yin-no //

94. bzaṅ-po bźi-po 'di-dag ni b. ch. s. dp. rnams-kyi mi-dge-ba'i grogs-po yin-par rig-par-bya-ste / bź. g. ź. n. / theg-pa-dman-pa ston-pa daṅ / byaṅ-chub-kyi[17] sems-la[18] 'dun-pa[19] zlog[20]-par-byed-pa daṅ / gaṅ-dag bsten-na mi-dge-ba'i chos[21] 'phel-bar-'gyur-ba daṅ / dge-ba'i chos-rnams las yoṅs-su-ñams-par-'gyur-ba-ste / bźi-po de-dag yin-no //

95. bzaṅ-po b. ch. s. dp. chos-bźi-daṅ-ldan-na saṅs-rgyas bcom-ldan-'das-rnams daṅ phrad-par-'gyur-te / bź. g. ź. n. / dran-pa rtse-gcig[22]-pa daṅ[23] / saṅs-rgyas bcom-ldan-'das-rnams-kyi

---

[1] P *ad.* yaṅ [2] c. Ch.; BP skyed, N bskyed [3] P 'dzin [4] N bzo [5] N *om.* byas-pa-tshor-ba daṅ [6] BP tu, N du [7] N gson [8] B rtsa N rtsa-la [9] BN *om.* bzaṅ-po [10] BP kyi [11] P 'phan [12] N cuṅ [13] N *om.* bźi-po [14] BP dpa' [15] BP sñen [16] B rton [17] B *om.* kyi [18] N *om.* [19] P par [20] N bzlog [21] N *ad* la [22] P cig [23] N *om.* dran-pa rtse-gcig-pa daṅ

bsṅags[1]-pa yaṅ daṅ yaṅ-du sgrogs-pa daṅ / tshul-khrims yoṅs-su-dag-pa daṅ / lhag-pa'i bsam-pas smon-lam 'debs-pa-ste / bźi-po de-dag yin-no //

96. bzaṅ-po b. ch. s. dpa'[2] phan-yon bźi-po 'di-dag mthoṅ-na / de-bźin-gśegs-pa-la mchod-pa-bya-bar spro-bar 'gyur-te / bź. g. ź. n. / yon-gnas mchog-la mchod-par-'gyur-ba daṅ / bdag mthoṅ-nas sems-can gźan-dag kyaṅ de-bźin-du mchod-pa byed-par 'gyur-ba-daṅ / de-bźin-gśegs-pa legs-par-mchod-nas[3] byaṅ-chub-kyi[4] sems brtan-par 'gyur-ba daṅ / skyes-bu chen-po'i mtshan-sum-cu[5]-rtsa-gñis-daṅ-ldan-pa mṅon-sum-du mthoṅ-na dge-ba'i rtsa-ba sogs[6]-par 'gyur-ba-ste / bzaṅ-po b. ch. s. dpa'[7] phan-yon bźi-po de-dag mthoṅ-na / de-bźin-gśegs-pa-la mchod-pa-bya-bar spro-bar 'gyur-ro //

97. bzaṅ-po de-bźin-du b. ch. s. dpas[8] don-gyi[9] dbaṅ bźi[10] mthoṅ-na bslab-pa lhur-len-par 'gyur-te / bź. g. ź. n. / ṅan-'gro-las yaṅ-dag-par-'da'-ba daṅ / bde-'gro 'thob[11]-par 'gyur-ba daṅ / de-bźin-gśegs-pa-la gus-pa daṅ / smon-lam yoṅs-su-rdzogs-par 'gyur-ba-ste / bźi-po de-dag yin-no //

98. bzaṅ-po bźi-po 'di-dag ni b. ch. s. dp.-rnams-kyi bslab-pa yin-te / bź. g. ź. n. / byaṅ-chub-kyi[12] sems mi-'dor-ba daṅ / sems-can thams-cad-la mñam-par-sbyor-ba daṅ / pha-rol-tu-phyin-pa yoṅs-su-tshol-ba daṅ / saṅs-rgyas-kyi chos tshad-med-pa mñam-pa-la mi-skrag-pa-ste / bzaṅ-po bźi-po de-dag ni b. ch. s. dp.-rnams-kyi[13] bslab-pa yin-no //

99. bzaṅ-po bźi-po 'di-dag ni b. ch. s. dp.-rnams-kyi bslab-pa yoṅs-su-dag-pa yin-te / bź. g. ź. n. / bya-ba-ma-yin-pa mi-spyod-pa daṅ / stoṅ-pa-ñid-la mos-pa daṅ / saṅs-rgyas-kyi byaṅ-chub mi-spoṅ-ba daṅ / lta-ba bag-la-ñal-ba daṅ bcas-par[14] yaṅ-dag-par 'joms-pa[15]-ste / bzaṅ-po bźi-po[16] de-dag ni b. ch. s. dp.-rnams-kyi bslab-pa yoṅs-su-dag-pa yin-no //

100. bzaṅ-po bźi-po 'di-dag ni b. ch. s. dp.-rnams-kyi tiṅ-ṅe[17]-'dzin-gyi[18] rigs yin-te / bź. g. ź. n. / 'du-'dzi-med-pa daṅ / rab-tu-dben-pa daṅ / sems-kyi rñog-pa-med-pa daṅ / dge-ba'i rtsa-ba

---

[1] P sṅags [2] P dpas [3] BP na [4] P *om.* kyi [5] BP bcu [6] B stsogs [7] BP dpas [8] BP dpa' [9] P gyis [10] N bźin [11] N thob [12] P *om.* kyi [13] B *inserts here the text omitted above (see p. 39 f. n. 7)*, P *repeats the same text.* [14] B *om.* par [15] N *om.* pa [16] N *om.* bźi-po [17] P *om.* ṅe [18] P kyi

ṅe-bar-rton[1]-pa-ste / bzaṅ-po bźi-po de[2]-dag ni b. ch. s. dp.-rnams-kyi tiṅ-ṅe-'dzin-gyi[3] rigs yin-no //

101. bzaṅ-po bźi-po 'di-dag ni b. ch. s. dp.-rnams-kyi tshul-bźin rab-tu-sbyor-ba yin-te / bź. g. ź. n. / dge-ba'i rtsa-ba bskyed-nas[4] byaṅ-chub-kyi sems mṅon-du-byed-pa daṅ / naṅ-du yaṅ-dag-'jog-pa-la sgrib-pa-med-pa daṅ / rnam-par-thar-ba'i[5] sgo-dag-la 'dris-par byed-pa daṅ / ṅes-pa-la mi-'jug-pa[6]-ste / bzaṅ-po bźi-po de[7]-dag ni b. ch. s. dp.-rnams-kyi tshul-bźin rab-tu[8]-sbyor-ba yin-no //

102. bzaṅ-po bźi-po[9] 'di-dag ni b. ch. s. dp.-rnams-kyi tshul-bźin-ma-yin-pa'i sems-skye-ba zlog[10]-par bya-ba yin-te / bź. g. ź. n. / 'khor-ba'i 'jigs-pas skrag-pa daṅ / rnal-'byor-spyod-pa-dag-la ma-mos-pa daṅ / dgoṅs[11]-pa-dag-la mi-dga'-ba daṅ / dge-ba'i rtsa-ba-rnams mṅon-par-'du-mi-byed-pa-ste / bzaṅ-po bźi-po de-dag ni tshul-bźin-ma-yin-pa'i sems-skye-ba zlog[10]-par bya-ba yin-no //

103. bzaṅ-po bźi-po 'di-dag ni b. ch. s. dp.-rnams-kyi sems-kyis ṅes-par-bsam-pa yin-te / bź. g. ź. n. / sems-can 'ga'i don-gyi phyir yaṅ bskal-pa phyi-ma'i mthar-thug-par 'khor-ba-na 'khor-bar bya'o sñam-pa 'di ni sems-kyis ṅes-par-bsam-pa daṅ-po yin-no // bdag-gis sems-can thams-cad-kyi sems-kyi spyod-pa-rnams śes-par-bya-źiṅ de-dag-gi ñon-moṅs-pa rab-tu-źi-bar bya-ba daṅ / dbaṅ-po-mchog daṅ mchog-ma-yin-pa śes-par-bya-ba'i phyir chos bstan-par-bya'o sñam-pa 'di ni sems-kyis ṅes-par-bsam-pa gñis-pa yin-no // bdag-gis[12] mi-dge-ba'i chos thams-cad spaṅs-śiṅ / dge-ba'i chos-thams-cad-daṅ-ldan-par byas-nas / byaṅ-chub-kyi sñiṅ-po-la 'dug-ste[13] / bdud-kyi dpuṅ pham-par byas-nas / bla-na-med-pa yaṅ-dag-par-rdzogs-pa'i byaṅ-chub mṅon-par-rdzogs-par 'tshaṅ-rgya-bar bya'o sñam-pa 'di ni sems-kyis ṅes-par-bsam-pa gsum-pa yin-no // stoṅ-gsum-gyi stoṅ-chen-po'i 'jig-rten-gyi khams skad-cig-gis go-bar-byas-te / chos bstan-par-bya'o sñam-pa 'di ni sems-kyis ṅes-par-bsam-pa bźi-pa yin-te / bzaṅ-po bźi-po de-dag ni b. ch. s. dp.-rnams-kyi sems-kyis[14] ṅes-par-bsam-pa yin-no //

104. bzaṅ-po chos bźi-po 'di[15]-dag ni[16] b. ch. s. dp.-rnams-kyi bdud-'dul-ba yin-te / bź. g. ź. n. / chos-la sgyu-ma lta-bur so-

---

[1] N ston [2] N 'di [3] P kyi [4] BP skyes-na [5] N dag-pa'i [6] N *om.* pa [7] N 'di [8] P du [9] B *om.* po [10] N bzlog [11] B dgos [12] B gi, P gas [13] N jug-go [14] B *om.* sems-kyis [15] B de [16] P na

sor-rtog-pa daṅ / tshul-bźin-du sbyor-ba daṅ / chos thams-cad-la rnam-par-mi-rtog-pa daṅ / mtshan-ma thams-cad-la mi-gnas-pa-ste / bzaṅ-po chos bźi-po de-dag ni bdud-'dul-ba yin-no //

105. bzaṅ-po bźi-po 'di-dag ni b. ch. s. dp.-rnams-kyi don-sems-pa yin-te / bź. g. ź. n. / gaṅ-zag-med-pa'i phyir chos-rnams rten-nas skye-ba yin-gyi / chos 'ga' yaṅ[1] rgyu-med-par[2] ni mi-skye-ba daṅ / rten-nas skyes-pa'i[3] chos gaṅ yin-pa de ma-skyes-pa daṅ / dṅos-po-med-pa daṅ / byaṅ-chub-kyi phyir chud-mi-za-ba-ste / bzaṅ-po bźi-po de-dag ni b. ch. s. dp.-rnams-kyi don-sems-pa yin-no //

106. bzaṅ-po b. ch. s. dp. chos-bźi-daṅ-ldan-na sems-can-rnams mi-gtoṅ-ba yin-te / bź. g. ź. n. / sṅon-gyi smon-lam mi-'dor-ba daṅ / yoṅs-su-skyo-ba bzod-pa daṅ / lus-daṅ-srog-la mi-lta-ba daṅ / bsdu-ba'i dṅos-pos sdud-pa-ste / bźi-po de-dag yin-no //

107. bzaṅ-po bźi-po 'di-dag-ni b. ch. s. dp.-rnams-kyi yoṅs-su-smin-par-byed-pa yin-te / bź. g. ź. n. / 'jig-rten-gyi zaṅ-ziṅ sbyin-pa yoṅs-su-gtoṅ-ba daṅ / yoṅs-su-smin-pa-la chos-ston-pa yoṅs-su-gtoṅ-ba daṅ[4] / dus-dus[5]-su skul[6]-bas dran-par-byed-pa yoṅs-su[7]-gtoṅ-ba daṅ / bdag-ñid-kyi bde-ba spaṅs-nas gźan-gyi dge[8]-ba'i rtsa-ba brten[9]-pa daṅ yoṅs-su-smin-par byed-pa-ste / bzaṅ-po bźi-po de-dag ni b. ch. s. dp.-rnams-kyi yoṅs-su-smin-par-byed-pa yin-no //

108. bzaṅ-po b. ch. s. dp. ch. bź. d. ld. na ma-bsdus-pa sdud-par-byed-pa-la mi-'jigs-pa yin-te / bź. g. ź. n. / dge-ba'i rtsa-ba chuṅ-du-la yaṅ mos-pa daṅ / rtag-tu rgyun mi-'chad-par gźan-gyi don byed-pa[10]-la[11] spro-ba daṅ / sbyin-pa daṅ dul-ba daṅ / ṅes-pa phun-sum-tshogs-pa daṅ / rñed-pa daṅ bkur-sti[12] daṅ / tshigs-su-bcad-pa thams-cad-la don-du gñer-ba-med-pa-ste / bźi-po de-dag yin-no //

109. bzaṅ-po b. ch. s. dp. ch. bź. d. ld. na sems-can-gyi spyod-pa-la 'jug-pa yin-te / bź. g. ź. n. / mṅon-par-śes-pa thob-pa daṅ / ye-śes thob-pa daṅ / tiṅ-ṅe-'dzin chen-por gyur-pa tshad-med-pa-la 'jug-pa daṅ / rnam-pa thams-cad-kyi mchog-daṅ-ldan-pa'i stoṅ-pa-ñid bsgom[13]-źiṅ rnam-par-grol-ba daṅ ma-'dres-pa-ste / bźi-po de-dag yin-no //

---

[1] B 'gag-pa *instead of* 'ga' yaṅ [2] N daṅ [3] P skye-ba'i, N skyes-pa daṅ rten-nas skyes-pa'i [4] B *om.* yoṅs-su-smin-pa-la chos-ston-pa yoṅs-su-gtoṅ-ba daṅ [5] N *om.* [6] N bskul [7] B *om.* su [8] N bde [9] NP ston [10] N par [11] N *om.* [12] N bsti [13] BP sgom

110. bzaṅ-po b. ch. s. dp. ch. bź. d. ld. na thabs-la-mkhas-pa yin-par rig-par-bya-ste / bź. g. ź. n. / sems-bskyed-pa thams-cad-la byaṅ-chub-kyi sems-sṅon-du-'gro-ste / tha-na ñon-moṅs-pa'i sems-la yaṅ ruṅ-na / dge-ba'i sems-la lta-smos kyaṅ ci dgos-pa daṅ / sems-can thams-cad chos-kyi snod-ñid yin-par lta-ba daṅ / ṅo-bo-ñid-med-par khoṅ-du-chud-pas chos-thams-cad log-pa-ñid-du ṅes-pa yin-par lta-ba daṅ / rnam-par-grol-ba-'dod-pas sñoms-par 'jug-pa thams-cad-la[1] mṅon-par-źen-pa-med-pa'i 'du-śes sgom-par-byed-pa-ste / b. ch. s. dp. chos-bźi-po-de-dag-daṅ-ldan-na thabs-la-mkhas-pa yin-par rig-par bya'o //

111. bzaṅ-po bźi-po 'di-dag ni b. ch. s. dp.-rnams-kyi byams-pa bsgom[2]-pa yin-te / bź. g. ź. n. / bdag-gis sems-can thams-cad-bskyab-par-bya'o / sñam-du byams-pa bsgom-pa daṅ / bdag-gis sems-can thams-cad bsgral-bar bya'o / sñam-du byams-pa bsgom-pa daṅ / bdag-gis sems-can thams-cad bskul-bar bya'o / sñam-du byams-pa bsgom[2]-pa daṅ / bdag-gis sems-can thams-cad yoṅs-su-mya-ṅan-las zla'o[3] / sñam-du byams-pa sgom-pa-ste / bzaṅ-po de-dag ni b. ch. s. dp.-rnams-kyi byams-pa bsgom-pa[2] yin-no //

112. bzaṅ-po bźi-po 'di-dag ni b. ch. s. dp.-rnams-kyi sñiṅ-rje yin-te / bź. g. ź. n. / ṅan-soṅ-du skyes-pa-rnams bde-'gro'i-lam-la 'god-pa'i sñiṅ-rje daṅ / sdig-pa'i las-daṅ-ldan-pa-rnams dge-ba'i chos-la sbyor-ba'i sñiṅ-rje daṅ / theg-pa-dman-pa-la mos-pa-rnams theg-pa-chen-po-la[4] yaṅ-dag-par-len-du-'jug-pa'i sñiṅ-rje daṅ / sems-can thams-cad yoṅs-su-mya-ṅan-las bzla'o sñam-pa'i sñiṅ-rje ni bźi-pa yin-te / bźi-po de-dag yin-no //

113. bzaṅ-po b. ch. s. dp. ch. bź. d. ld. na mṅon-par-śes-pa 'thob-par-'gyur-te / bź. g. ź. n. / lus daṅ sems yaṅ-ba daṅ / sgyu-ma'i raṅ-bźin-du rnam-par-'byed-pa daṅ / sems-can thams-cad-la gus-pa daṅ rim-gro'i[5] sems-bskyed-pa daṅ / źi-gnas[6]-la rtse-gcig[7]-tu-gyur-pas rnam-par-gyeṅ-ba-med-pa yin-no //

114. bzaṅ-po b. ch. s. dp. ch. bź. d. ld. na so-so-yaṅ-dag-par-rig-pa[8] 'thob-par[9]-'gyur-te / bź. g. ź. n. / don-la rton-pa-yin-gyi tshig[10]-'bru-la mi-rton-pa daṅ / chos-la rton-pa yin-gyi gaṅ-zag-la mi-rton-pa daṅ / chos thams-cad bdag-med-pa'i ṅes-pa'i tshig daṅ /

---

[1] N *om.* [2] BP sgom [3] N 'da'-bar-bya'o *instead of* zla'o [4] BP *om.* la [5] P 'gro'i [6] P nas [7] P cig [8] NP par [9] NP pa [10] N chig

yi-ge mi-zad-par śes-nas chags-pa-med-ciṅ thogs-pa-med-par ston-pas ston-par-byed-pa-ste / bźi-po de-dag yin-no //

115. bzaṅ-po b. ch. s. dp. ch. bź. d. ld.-na gzuṅs 'thob-par-'gyur-te / bź. g. ź. n. / maṅ-du-thos-pas ṅoms[1]-mi-śes-pa daṅ / maṅ du-thos-pa-rnams-la chos bźin-du[2] gus-par bsñen-bkur-byed-pa daṅ / rtag-tu gźan-dag-la chos-ston-par brtson-pa daṅ / tshig daṅ yi-ge thams-cad gtan-la dbab-pa'i phyir de-bźin-gśegs-pa'i dgoṅs-te gsuṅs-pa-la[3] 'jug-pa yin-no //

116. bzaṅ-po b. ch. s. dp. ch. bź. d. ld.-na bzod-pa-'thob-par-'gyur-te / bź. g. ź. n. / mos-pa daṅ / phyir-mi-ldog-pa daṅ / tshogs daṅ / yoṅs-su-mi-skyo-ba-ste / bźi-po de-dag yin-no //

117. bzaṅ-po b. ch. s. dp. ch. bź. d. ld.-na spobs-pa dag-pa[4] 'thob-par-'gyur-te // bź. g. ź. n. / chos-smra-ba gźan[5]-dag-gis bśad-pa daṅ 'gal-bar mi-byed-pa daṅ[6] / chos-smra-ba-la gus-pa daṅ bcas-śiṅ źe-sa daṅ bcas-par chos ñan-pa daṅ / thos-pas kheṅs-pa-med-pa daṅ / thos-pa ñuṅ-ṅu-rnams-la brñas-par mi-byed-pa-ste / bźi-po de-dag yin-no //

118. bzaṅ-po bźi-po 'di-dag-ni b. ch. s. dp. rnams-kyi bsgyur-ba-ste / bź. g. ź. n. / 'dod-chags daṅ źe-sdaṅ daṅ gti-mug bsgyur-ba daṅ / ñan-thos-las bsgyur-ba daṅ / raṅ-saṅs-rgyas-las bsgyur-ba daṅ / dge-ba'i rtsa-ba'i[7] chos-la 'du-śes bsgyur-ba-ste / bźi-po de-dag yin-no //

119. bzaṅ-po chos bźi-po 'di-dag-ni b. ch. s. dp. rnams-kyi don zab-mo-la sbyor-ba yin-te / bź. g. ź. n. / rten-ciṅ-'brel-bar-'gyur-bar rtogs-par-byed-pa daṅ / dgoṅs-pa rtogs[8]-par-byed-pa daṅ / bdag-gi ṅo-bo-ñid rtogs-par-byed-pa daṅ / 'di-ltar stoṅ-pa'i don-du chos de-dag thams-cad[9] don-gcig[10]-par rtogs[11]-par-byed-pa-ste / bźi-po de-dag ni b. ch. s. dp. rnams-kyi zab-mo-la sbyor-ba yin-no //

120. bzaṅ-po b. ch. s. dp. ch. bź. d. ld. na smon-lam 'grub-par-'gyur-te / bź. g. ź. n. / tshul-khrims daṅ bslab-pa yoṅs-su-dag-pa daṅ / las-kyi sgrib-pa rnam-par[12]-sbyoṅ-ba daṅ / gyo-sgyu-med-pa daṅ / dge-ba'i rtsa-ba bskyed-pa-la sems-dpa'[13]-byed-pa-ste / bźi-po de-dag ni b. ch. s. dp. rnams-kyi smon-lam 'grub-par-'gyur-ba'o //

121. bzaṅ-po b. ch. s. dp. chos. bź. d. ld. na pha-rol-tu-phyin-pa thams-cad-kyis 'phags-śiṅ phyir-mi-ldog-pa'i chos-can-du 'gyur-

[1] B doms [2] N *om.* du [3] BP *om.* la 'jug-pa [4] N *om.* pa
[5] N *ad.* de [6] B ste [7] B ba [8] BP rtog [9] B *om.* cad [10] P cig
[11] P rtog [12] N yoṅs-su [13] B dbaṅ

te / bź. g. ź. n. / thabs-mkhas-pa-daṅ-ldan-pas pha-rol-tu-phyin-pa gcig-gi naṅ-du pha-rol-tu-phyin-pa gźan thams-cad kyaṅ sdud-par byed-pa daṅ / thabs-mkhas-pa-daṅ-ldan-pas sems-can gcig-gi[1] raṅ-bźin rtogs-pas de-las gźan-pa'i sems-can thams-cad kyaṅ śes-pa daṅ / thabs-mkhas-pa-daṅ-ldan-pas chos rnam-par-dag-pa gcig-gi tshul rtogs-pas chos gźan-dag-gi rnam-par-dag-pa yaṅ śes-pa daṅ / chos-ñid yin-pas saṅs-rgyas thams-cad[2] saṅs-rgyas gcig-tu mos-pa-ste / bzaṅ-po b. ch. s. dp. chos. bźi-po de-dag-daṅ-ldan-na pha-rol-tu-phyin-pa thams-cad-kyis 'phags-śiṅ phyir-mi-ldog-pa'i chos-can-du 'gyur-ro //

122. bcom-ldan-'das-kyis bźi-po[3] bsgrub-pa 'di bśad-pa-na / sgyu-ma-mkhan bzaṅ-po mi-skye-ba'i chos-la bzod-pa thob-nas tshim-źiṅ mgu-la yid[4]-raṅs-te / rab-tu-dga'-źiṅ dga'-ba daṅ / yid bde-bar gyur-nas / dga'-ba daṅ mchog-tu-dga'-ba de-ñid-kyis / śiṅ ta[5]-la bdun srid tsam-gyi steṅ-gi nam-mkha'-la 'phags-so // de-nas bcom-ldan-'das-kyis de'i tshe 'dzum-pa mdzad-do // 'dzum-pa mdzad-pa'i źal-gyi sgo-nas 'od-zer graṅs-med dpag-tu-med-pa bkye-nas[6] saṅs-rgyas-kyi źiṅ thams-cad 'od-zer des khyab-par byas-nas / slar yaṅ bcom-ldan-'das-kyi[7] dbu'i gtsug-tu nub-bo // de-nas tshe-daṅ-ldan-pa kun-dga'-bo stan-las laṅs-te / chos-gos phrag-pa gcig-tu bgos-nas pus-mo gyas-pa'i lha-ṅa sa-la bcugs[8]-te / bcom-ldan-'das ga-la-ba-de logs-su thal-mo sbyar-ba btud-nas / bcom-ldan-'das-la 'di-skad ces gsol-to // btsun[9]-pa bcom-ldan-'das de-bźin-gśegs-pa ni rgyu-ma-mchis-pa daṅ / rkyen-ma-mchis-par 'dzum-pa mi-mdzad-na / 'dzum-pa mdzad-pa'i rgyu gaṅ lags rkyen gaṅ lags / de'i tshe tshigs-su bcad-pa 'di-dag kyaṅ gsol-to //

123. ye-śes 'byuṅ-gnas gzi-brjid gźal-yas śes-rab-grags
'jig-rten gsum-du yon-tan pha-rol-phyin-brñes grags
rgyal-ba raṅ-byuṅ gaṅ-gi slad-du 'dzum-pa[10] bstan[11]
mi-yi dbaṅ-pos[12] de ni bdag-la bka'-stsal gsol

124. phyogs-rnams-na ni 'gro-bar sems-can ji-sñed gnas
de-dag kun-gyi[13] sems-kyi spyod-pa-rnams daṅ ni
dman daṅ mchog daṅ tha-ma bar-ma rgyu-ldan-mkhyen
ci[14]-slad 'dzum-pa mdzad-pa'i bdag-la bstan-du gsol

---

[1] NP gis [2] N *om.* saṅs-rgyas thams-cad [3] P pa [4] N yi [5] P rta [6] BP bas [7] B kyis [8] BP btsugs [9] N bcun [10] N *om.* pa [11] N bstan-pa [12] BP po [13] P kyi [14] B ci'i

125. lha daṅ de-bźin źugs 'bar-sgra ni gaṅ lags daṅ
mi-'am-ci daṅ mi daṅ brgya-byin lha-min daṅ
mkha'-ldiṅ lto-'phye[1] tshaṅs-pa'i sgra daṅ sgra gźan-rnams
saṅs-rgyas rdul-bral gsuṅ sgra'i char yaṅ ga-la phod[2]

126. 'od-bzaṅ ñi-ma'i 'od daṅ nor-bu 'od-rnams daṅ
brgya-byin 'od daṅ tshaṅs-pa'i 'od-rnams ji-sñed-pa
ji-ltar saṅs-rgyas 'od-kyis khyab-par gda'-ba ltar
'od-rnams de-dag thams-cad rnam-par-gsal ma-lags

127. saṅs-rgyas źiṅ de zab-mo'i chos ni rjes-su-thob
stoṅ-pa bdag-med sems-can gaṅ-zag-med mkhyen-nas
yod daṅ med-pa'i mtha'-gñis rnam-par-spaṅs-nas-su
dus gsum chu zla 'dra-bar rab-tu-mkhyen-pa-po

128. deṅ 'dir su-źig theg-pa'i mchog-la sems btud-te
su-źig saṅs-rgyas rigs daṅ chos-kyi rigs-la gnas
su-źig dkon-mchog-gsum-po rgya-chen skyed-par bgyid
gaṅ-gi ched-du 'dzum-pa-mdzad-pa legs-par-gsuṅs

129. gal-te rgyal-ba ñan-thos-rnams-la don-ldan gsuṅ
de tshe bde-gśegs 'dzum-pa źabs-kyi pus-mor nub
gal-te rkyen-gyi[3] theg-pa gsuṅ-na phrag-par nub
gaṅ-tshe[4] saṅs-rgyas-theg gsuṅ[5] de tshe spyi-bor nub

130. ji-ltar khyod-kyis 'od-zer 'bum sñed[6] rab-btaṅ-ba
bde-bar-gśegs-pa'i[7] gtsug-tu[8] nub-par-gyur-lags-na
phan mdzad lha-yi-lha-ste phan-pa-mdzad-pa-po
'dir ni saṅs-rgyas-theg-pa[9] luṅ-bstan[10] dogs[11] ma-mchis

131. de-nas bcom-ldan-'das-kyis tshe-daṅ-ldan-pa kun-dga'-bo-la bka'-stsal-pa / kun-dga'-bo khyod-kyis rigs-kyi[12] bu bzaṅ-po mthoṅ-ṅam // gsol-pa / bcom-ldan-'das mthoṅ-lags-so // bka'-stsal-pa / kun-dga'-bo rigs-kyi bu bzaṅ-po 'di ni bskal-pa dgu-khri ñi stoṅ 'das-pa[13]-na / bskal-pa legs-par-sprul-pa-la / 'jig-rten-gyi khams-bkod-pa chen-por / de-bźin-gśegs-pa dgra-bcom-pa yaṅ-dag-par rdzogs-pa'i saṅs-rgyas rnam-par-'phrul-ba'i-rgyal-po źes bya-bar 'jig-rten-du[14] 'byuṅ-bar 'gyur-ro[15] // kun-dga'-bo[16] de-bźin-

---

[1] P phye [2] c. Ch.; Mss. spyod [3] P kyi [4] P gal-te [5] N gsuṅs [6] BP sñiṅ [7] BP kyi [8] P du [9] BP par [10] BP ston [11] NP dgos [12] B *om.* kyi [13] NP *om.* 'das-pa [14] P du du [15] BP te [16] N *om.* kun-dga'-bo

gśegs-pa dgra-bcom-pa yaṅ-dag-par-rdzogs-pa'i saṅs-rgyas rnam-par-'phrul-ba'i-rgyal-po de'i 'jig-rten-gyi khams bkod-pa-chen-po de ni 'byor-bar 'gyur / rgyas-pa daṅ bde-ba daṅ / lo-legs-pa daṅ / ñams dga'-ba daṅ / mi daṅ skye-bo maṅ-pos gaṅ-bar 'gyur-źiṅ / lag-mthil ltar mñam-pa daṅ / ka-tsa-lin[1]-di[2] ltar reg-na 'dzam-pa daṅ / me-tog-gi siṅ-ljon-pas brgyan-pa daṅ / rol-mo sna-tshogs sgrogs-pa daṅ / spos sna-tshogs-kyis[3] bdugs-pa daṅ / rtag-tu rgyun mi-'chad-par gdugs daṅ / rgyal-mtshan daṅ / ba-dan bsgreṅ-bar 'gyur-ro // kun-dga'-bo bza'-ba daṅ / btuṅ-ba ni dper-na sum-cu-rtsa-gsum-pa'i lha-rnams-kyi loṅs-spyod-pa ltar bsam-pa tsam-gyis[4] 'grub-ste / mi de-dag-gi ñe-bar-spyad-pa daṅ / yoṅs-su-spyad-pa ni de-lta-bur 'gyur-ro // kun-dga'-bo de'i tshe 'jig-rten-gyi khams bkod-pa-chen-po rtag-tu bkod-pa[5] thams-cad ñe-bar-ston-par-byed-de / des-na[6] 'jig-rten-gyi khams de bkod-pa-chen-po źes bya'o // kun-dga'-bo saṅs-rgyas-kyi źiṅ der sems-can gaṅ-dag skyes-pa de-dag thams-cad kyaṅ rgya-chen-po-la mos-pa / theg-pa-chen-po-la yaṅ-dag-par-źugs-pa śa-stag-tu[7] 'gyur-ro // kun-dga'-bo de-bźin-gśegs-pa rnam-par-'phrul-ba'i-rgyal-po'i tshe[8]-tshad ni lo-khrir 'gyur-ro // yoṅs-su-mya-ṅan-las-'das-nas[9] kyaṅ dam-pa'i chos lo bye-bar gnas-par 'gyur-ro // kun-dga'-bo gaṅ-gi tshe de-bźin-gśegs-pa rnam-par-'phrul-ba'i-rgyal-po yoṅs-su-mya-ṅan-las-'da'-ba[10] de'i tshe yaṅ byaṅ-chub-sems-dpa' sgra-rnam-par-grags-pa 'di de'i 'og-tu de-bźin-gśegs-pa dgra-bcom-pa yaṅ-dag-par-rdzogs-pa'i saṅs-rgyas / kun-gyi[11]-khyab-bdag ces bya-bar 'jig-rten-du byuṅ-bar 'gyur-ro źes / byaṅ-chub-sems-dpa' sgra-rnam-par-grags[12]-pa luṅ-bstan-nas yoṅs-su-mya-ṅan-las-'da'o //

132. de-nas rigs-kyi-bu bzaṅ-po bar-snaṅ de-las babs-nas / bcom-ldan-'das-kyi źabs-la mgo-bos phyag-'tsal-te / bcom-ldan-'das-la 'di-skad ces gsol-to // bcom-ldan-'das bdag[13] deṅ slan-chad de-bźin-gśegs-pa dgra-bcom-pa yaṅ-dag-par-rdzogs-pa'i saṅs-rgyas bye-ba 'bum-phrag du-ma daṅ / chos daṅ dge-sloṅ-gi dge 'dun-la skyabs-su mchi'o // de-bźin-gśegs-pa[14] de-bźin-ñid gaṅ-gis de-bźin-ñid-las slar-ma-log-pa de-bźin-gśegs-pa'i de-bźin-ñid daṅ / dbyer-ma-mchis-pa'i de-bźin-ñid daṅ / ma-tshaṅ-ba-ma-mchis-pa'i de-bźin-ñid daṅ / rnam-par-mi-rtog-pa'i de-bźin-ñid daṅ / skye-ba-

---

[1] B li [2] BN 'di, P da [3] P kyi [4] P kyís [5] N *om.* bkod-pa
[6] B de-na, P de-nas [7] P du [8] N tshe'i [9] BP *om.* [10] NP 'das-pa
[11] P kyí [12] N grag [13] N bdag-gis [14] B pa'i

ma-mchis-pa'i de-bźin-ñid daṅ / mṅon-par-'du-bgyid-pa-ma-mchis-pa'i de-bźin-ñid-kyis / de-bźin-gśegs-pa'i [1] de-bźin-ñid gsuṅ-ba bźin-du bdag kyaṅ de-skad mchi'o //

133. de-nas tshe-daṅ-ldan-pa kun-dga'-bos rigs-kyi-bu bzaṅ-po-la 'di-skad ces smras-so // bzaṅ-po khyod de-bźin-gśegs-pa'i chos-ñid rjes-su-thob-pa'am ci-na / khyod ji-ltar de-bźin-gśegs-pa de-bźin-ñid gsuṅ-ba ltar khyod de-skad smra // bzaṅ-pos smras-pa / kun-dga'-bo chos thams-cad kyaṅ de-bźin-gśegs-pa'i chos-ñid thob-pa yin-no / de ci'i phyir źe-na / kun-dga'-bo 'di-ltar de-bźin-gśegs-pas de-bźin-ñid dbyer-med-pa-ñid-du thugs-su chud-de / de-bźiṅ-ñid dbyer-med-pa gaṅ yin-pa der kho-bo yaṅ chud-ciṅ / ji-ltar kho-bo chud-pa de [2]-bźin-du sem-can thams-cad kyaṅ chud-la [3] / ji-ltar sems-can thams-cad chud-pa de-bźin-du chos [4] thams-cad kyaṅ chud-pa'i phyir-te / btsun-pa kun-dga'-bo de-bźin-gśegs-pa'i chos-ñid ni gñis-kyis rab-tu-phye-ba ma-yin-no / btsun-pa kun-dga'-bo gñis-su-med-pa ni / gaṅ-na kun-tu-śes-pa-med-pa-ñid daṅ / yoṅs-su-śes-pa-med-pa-ñid-do / de ci'i phyir źe-na / 'du-śes yoṅs-su-śes-pa'i śes-pa ni saṅs-rgyas-kyi ye-śes yin-pa'i phyir-ro // de-nas bcom-ldan-'das-la tshe-daṅ-ldan-pa kun-dga'-bos 'di-skad ces gsol-to // bcom-ldan-'das rigs-kyi-bu bzaṅ-po ni lha daṅ bcas-pa'i 'jig-rten mgo-rmoṅs-par bgyid-pa-ste / sṅon yaṅ sgyu-ma'i chos-ñid-kyis mgo-rmoṅs-par bgyis-so // de yaṅ śes-rab daṅ ye-śes-kyis mgo-rmoṅs-par bgyid-do // de ci'i slad-du źe-na / di'i śes-rab daṅ / ye-śes-kyi spobs-pa ni de-lta-bu lags-pa'i slad-du'o //

134. de-nas bcom-ldan-'das-kyis sgyu-ma-mkhan bzaṅ-po-la 'di-skad ces bka'-stsal-to // bzaṅ-po khyod lha daṅ bcas-pa'i 'jig-rten mgo-rmoṅs-par byed-pa bden-nam [5] // gsol-ba / bcom-ldan-'das-kyis ji-ltar mgo-rmoṅs-par mdzad-pa de-bźin-du bdag kyaṅ mgo-rmoṅs-par-bgyid lags-so // de ci'i slad-du źe-na / bcom-ldan-'das 'di-lta-ste / bdag-med-pa-ñid-kyis sems-can-du tha-sñad btags-te / chos ston-pa daṅ / srog-med-pa daṅ / gaṅ-zag-med-pa-ñid-kyis gaṅ-zag-tu [6] chos ston-pa 'di ni mgo-rmoṅs-par-bgyid-pa chen-po lags-pa'i slad-du'o // de-bźin-gśegs-pas ni byaṅ-chub-kyi sñiṅ-po-la bźugs-nas chos 'ga' yaṅ 'chi-'pho-ba'am / 'gro-ba'am / skye-ba ma [7]-gzigs mod-kyi / 'chi-'pho-ba [8] daṅ / 'gro-ba daṅ / skye-ba'i cohs ston-par yaṅ [9] mdzad-de // bcom-ldan-'das de-lta lags-pas de-bźin-

---

[1] N pa [2] N *om.* de [3] BP *ad.* ji-ltar sems-can thams-cad kyaṅ chud-la
[4] N cheṣ [5] B nas [7] P du [1] N mi [8] B 'phos-pa, N 'pho [9] B *om.* yaṅ

gśegs-pa yaṅ-dag-par gsuṅ bka'-stsol[1]-ba ltar[2] lha daṅ bcas-pa'i 'jig-rten-gyi yul ga-la lags // de-nas bcom-ldan-'das-kyis sgyu-ma-mkhan bzaṅ-po-la legs-so źes bya-ba byin-te / rigs-kyi-bu legs-so / legs-so // khyod ci-skad[3] smra-ba de-kho-na bźin-te / 'di-lta-ste / bdag-med-pa-ñid-kyis sems-can-du tha-sñad btags-te / chos ston-pa daṅ / srog-med-pa daṅ / gaṅ-zag-med-pa-ñid-kyis gaṅ-zag-tu[4] chos[5] ston-pa 'di ni mgo-rmoṅs-pa chen-po yin-no // de-bźin-gśegs-pas ni byaṅ-chub-kyi sñiṅ-po-la bźugs-nas / chos 'ga' yaṅ 'chi-'pho-ba'am / 'gro-ba'am / skye-ba ma-gzigs mod-kyi / 'chi-'pho-ba daṅ / 'gro-ba daṅ / skye-ba'i chos ston-par yaṅ[6] mdzad-de / 'di-la yoṅs-su-mya-ṅan-las[7]-'da'-ba'am[8] / yoṅs-su-mya-ṅan-las-bzla-ba'i phyir chos-bstan[9]-pa'i chos ni 'ga' yaṅ med-do //

135. de-nas rigs-kyi bu bzaṅ-pos / bcom-ldan-'das-la rab-tu-'byuṅ-bar gsol-pa daṅ / bcom-ldan-'das-kyis byaṅ-chub-sems-dpa' byams-pa-la bka'-stsal-pa // byams-pa khyod-kyis rigs-kyi bu bzaṅ-po rab-tu-phyuṅ[10]-śig / de-nas byams-pas rigs-kyi bu bzaṅ-po rab-tu-phyuṅ-rdzogs[11]-par bsñen[12]-par[13]-byas-so // rab-tu-phyuṅ-rdzogs-par bsñen-nas kyaṅ / bcom-ldan-'das-la 'di-skad ces gsol-to // bcom-ldan-'das byaṅ-chub-sems-dpa'-rnams ni kha-dog daṅ / rtags-daṅ / tshul-gyis rab-tu-'byuṅ-ba ma-lags-so // bcom-ldan-'das de ci'i slad-du źe-na / byaṅ-chub-sems-dpa' gaṅ-źig mtshan-ma thams-cad-la yaṅ chags-pa ma-mchis-la / sems-can yoṅs-su-smin-par-bgyi-ba'i slad-du khams-gsum-na[14] yaṅ gnas-na[15] / de ni byaṅ-chub-sems-dpa'-rnams-kyi rab-tu-'byuṅ-ba lags-so // yaṅ de'i tshe bstan-pa 'di bśad-pa-na / srog-chags lṅa-stoṅ-gis ni bla-na-med-pa yaṅ-dag-par-rdzogs-pa'i byaṅ-chub-tu[4] sems bskyed-do // dge-sloṅ ñi[16]-brgya ni len-pa-med-par zag-pa-rnams-las sems rnam-par-grol-lo //

136. de-nas bcom-ldan-'das-la tshe-daṅ-ldan-pa kun-dga'-bos 'di-skad ces gsol-to // bcom-ldan-'das chos-kyi rnam-graṅs 'di'i miṅ[17] ci lags / 'di'i miṅ ji-skad ces gzuṅ-bar-bgyi // bcom-ldan-'das-kyis bka'-stsal-pa / sgyu-ma-mkhan bzaṅ-po luṅ-bstan-pa[18] źes bya-bar[19] zuṅ[20]-śig / rim-gyis byaṅ-chub-yaṅ-dag-par-'byuṅ źes bya-bar yaṅ zuṅ[20]-śig / kun-dga'-bo byaṅ-chub-sems-dpa' gaṅ de-bzin-gśegs-pa blta-bar 'dod-pa daṅ / sems-can-rnams-la saṅs-rgyas-kyi

---

[1] P stsal [2] BP lta [3] BP *om.* [4] P du [5] BP *om.* [6] B *om.* yaṅ [7] B *om.* las [8] BP 'das-pa'am [9] BP ston [10] B phyuṅs [11] N *om.* rdzogs [12] N *ad.* rdzogs [13] B pa [14] B na [15] P mi gnas na [16] N ñis [17] BP mi [18] B *om.* pa [19] N *ad.* yaṅ [20] B zuṅs

mdzad-par-bya-bar 'dod-pa des chos-kyi rnam-grañs 'di gzuñ-bar-bya / bcañ-bar-bya / bklag[1]-par-bya / gźan-dag-la yañ bstan-par bya'o // de ci'i phyir źe-na / kun-dga'-bo gañ-gis 'di bzuñ[2]-ba dañ / bcañ[3]-ba dañ / bklags-pa dañ / gźan-dag-la yañ rab-tu-bstan-pa des ni de-bźin-gśegs-pa[4] mthoñ-ba yin / des ni sems-can-rnams-la sañs-rgyas-kyi mdzad-pa yañ byas-pa yin-no / kun-dga'-bo de-lta-bas-na / khyod-kyis skye-bo mañ-po-la bde-ba dañ / 'jig-rten-la sñiñ-brtse-ba dañ / 'di-lta-ste lha dañ mi-rnams-kyi don dañ / phan-pa dañ bde-ba'i phyir / chos-kyi rnam-grañs 'di zuñ[5]-śig / choñs[6]-śig / lhogs-śig / kun-chub-par-gyis-śig / kun-dga'-bo chos gañ-dag-gis byañ-chub yañ-dag-par-'byuñ-bar[7] 'gyur-ba / de-dag ni[8] theg-pa-chen-po 'di-las yañ-dag-par-'byuñ-ba[9] de-dag ni theg-pa-chen-po 'di-las yañ-dag-par rab-tu-ston-te / des-na chos-kyi rnam-grañs 'di ni[10] byañ-chub yañ-dag-par[11]-'byuñ-ba źes bya'o // kun-dga'-bo khyod mos-par-bya'o // khoñ-du chud-par bya'o / gañ-źig chos-kyi rnam-grañs 'di glegs-bam-du byed-pa'am / lus-la srel[12]-ba / de'i lus-la de-bźin-gśegs-pa yod-pa yin-na / gañ-dag-gis thos-nas de-bźin-ñid-du sgrub[13]-pa lta-smos kyañ ci-dgos //

137. de-nas bcom-ldan-'das-la / rigs-kyi-bu bzañ-pos 'di-skad ces gsol-to // bcom-ldan-'das chos-kyi rnam-grañs 'di ni sñon-kyi dge-ba'i rtsa-ba bskul-ba źes bgyi lags-so // de ci'i slad-du źe-na / bcom-ldan-'das 'di-ltar bdag-gis chos-kyi rnam-grañs 'di thos-nas dge-ba'i rtsa-ba sñon-bsags-pa thams-cad mñon-sum-du gyur-pa'i slad-du lags-so // bcom-ldan-'das-kyis de-skad ces bka'-stsal-nas / rigs-kyi-bu bzañ-po[14] dañ / tshe-dañ-ldan-pa kun-dga'-bo dañ thams-cad-dañ-ldan-pa'i 'khor de-dag dañ / lha dañ / mi-dañ / lha-ma-yin dañ / dri-zar bcas-pa'i 'jig-rten yid[15]-rañs-te // bcom-ldan-'das-kyi[16] gsuñs-pa-la mñon-par-stod-do //

'phags-pa-dkon-mchog-brtsegs-pa chen-po'i chos-kyi rnam-grañs le'u stoñ-phrag brgya-pa[17] // sgyu-ma-mkhan bzañ-po luñ-bstan-pa źes bya-ste // 'dus[18] ñi-śu-rtsa-gcig-pa rdzogs-so //

---

[1] BP klag [2] B gzuñ [3] N bcañs [4] BP pas [5] B zuñs [6] P chañs [7] BP ba dañ [8] BP *om.* 'gyur-ba de-dag ni [9] BP bar *and ad.* 'gyur-ba [10] N *om.* [11] B *om.* par [12] N bsrel [13] N bsgrub [14] B pos [15] N yi [16] N kyis [17] N *ad.* las [18] P le'u *for* 'dus

TRANSLATION

Homage to all the Buddhas and Bodhisattvas

1. Thus have I heard: — The Lord was once staying at Rājagṛha on Vulture's Peak Hill with a large assembly of 1250 monks and 5000 Bodhisattvas Mahāsattvas[43], highly renowned[44], possessed of supernatural faculties[45], knowers of spells[46], endowed with miraculous power[47], having reached the acceptance of the doctrine that all the *dharmas* are without origination[48], such as the Bodhisattvas Mahāsattvas Siṃha, Siṃhamati, Sucandana, Sārathi, Mahāsārathi, Prabhāśrī, Prabhākara[49], Prabhātejas Prīya-

---

[43] Ch_1 om. *mahāsattva*, Ch_2: »with 1250 monks, with a group of Arhats knowing all what is to be known and 5000 Bodhisattvas-Mahāsattvas (of course the reading »5000« attested by the »Three editions« must be substituted to the reading »50« adopted by the Taishō editors).

[44] Ch_2 om. Ch_1 also om. but inserts after »possessed of supernatural faculties« *ta sheng hsi* »very noble« which seem to correspond to this T. epithet.

[45] *abhijñā*

[46] *dhāraṇī*

[47] *ṛddhiprātihārya*. Ch_1: »which attained the *dhāraṇīs* and the *asaṅgapratibhāna*«. We have here an obvious confusion of *prātihārya* with *pratibhāna* and it is not unlikely that the reading of Ch_1, though preserved in this version only, is the better one. *asaṅgapratibhāna* is very usual in such »clichés«, cf. *e. g.* the beginning of the *Rāṣṭrapālaparipṛcchā*.

[48] *anutpattikadharmakṣānti*, see Suzuki, *Studies on Laṅkāvatāra*, p. 126 ff. and Har Dayal, *The Bodhisattva Doctrine*, London 1932, p. 213.

Ch_2 translates the whole sentence as follows: »the Bodh.-Mah. who attained the *ṛddhiprātihārya*, acquired the *anutpattikadharmakṣānti* and the *dhāraṇis*.«

[49] Ch_1: *kuang ching* corresponds rather to *Prabhāśuddha*.

svara[50], Prabhāvyūha[51], Prakāśabuddhi[52], Sattvasāra[53], Sattvasārathi Vinayavān[54], and all the Bhadrakalpika Bodhisattvas Mahāsattvas[55] to begin with Maitreya and Mañjuśrī, as prince royal. Those 5000 Bodhisattvas Mahāsattvas headed by the afore-mentioned were sitting together and were surrounded: by Śakra, the ruler of gods[56], by Brahma Sahāṃpati[57], by the four Great Kings and many gods, *nāgas*[58], *yakṣas, asuras, garuḍas*[59], *gandharvas, kinnaras* and *mahoragas.*

2. And[60] whilst the Lord was staying in the great town of Rājagṛha, the king[61], the great ministers, the brahmins[62], the householders and the people of the city and of the whole country[63] showed him respect and reverence, adored and worshipped him, offered him robes, food, implements of bedding and sitting and medicinal appliances for use in sickness[64].

3. And they all exalted in extensive verses the glory and

---

[50] Both Ch. om. the surname *Prīyasvara.* As for *Prabhātejas* this name is attested by T. and Ch_2. Ch_1 has *chi i* = *Śāntamati.*

[51] Ch_1 om.

[52] This reconstruction is very doubtful. In Mhv. (5033) *dhaivata* corresponds to T. *blo-gsal* but this is the name of a gamut. Ch_1: *jen ming,* Ch_2: *ming chio.*

[53] Ch_1: *k'ai hua jen* = *sattvaparipācana* (see foot-note 523), Ch_2: *chung shang,* which can render *sattvasāra,* but which rather would correspond to *saṃghavara.*

[54] Both Ch. om. the surname *Vinayavaān.* As for *Sattvasārathi* Ch_1 has the equivalent *ch'ang ying* which is difficult to explain. Would it mean: »who always fulfils [the wishes of beings]«? Ch_2 om.

[55] Ch_1: »60 Bhadrakalpikas«.

[56] Ch_1 om. this epithet, and Ch_2 renders *devānām indra* by the phonetic transcription *t'i huan yin.*

[57] Ch_1 om. *Sahāṃpati,* Ch_2 renders it by *so p'o shih chieh chu.*

[58] Ch_1: »innumerable *nāgarājas* and gods *(shen)*«. § 1 of Ch_1 ends here.

[59] Ch_2 om.

[60] In Ch_2 §§ 2 and 3 are interchanged.

[61] Ch_2: »The king of the country of Rājagṛha«.

[62] Ch_1: »burgess« *(ch'ang che* = *śreṣṭhin).* This word very often occurs together with *gṛhapati,* cf. *e. g. seṭṭhi gahapati, Vin.* I, 273, *Sam. Nik.* I, 92, etc. In the § 32 of Ch_1 *ch'ang che* corresponds to *gṛhapati.*

[63] Ch_1: »all the officials«, Ch_2: »all the people«.

[64] *cīvara, āhāra, śayanāsana, glānapratyayabhaiṣajya.* Ch_1 interchanges the last two points, Ch_2 interchanges the first two points.

the laud of the Lord[65], calling him the Tathāgata, the Arhat, the Fully Enlightened One, Endowed with Wisdom and Virtue, the Sugata, the Knower of the World, the Supreme Guide of men who have to be restrained, the Teacher of gods and men, the Buddha and the Lord, Omniscient and All-seeing[66], as he knows and sees everything[67], endowed with ten powers of the Tathāgata[68], with four grounds of self-confidence[68], with four kinds of comprehensions[70], with eighteen uncommon properties of the Buddha[71], with great benevolence and great compassion[72], enjoying the untroubled sight of Buddha[73], possessed of the 5 kinds of clairvoyance[74], endowed with miraculous powers[75] such as: wonders of speech, wonders of teaching and wonders of magic[76], and being able to uphold in the skies, on part of the point of a hair, all the Great Universe with towns, cities, the whole earth[77], the living world[78], the mount Sumeru, the

---

[65] Ch_1: »The glory of the Lord reached far away«, Ch_2: »The glory of the Lord Tathāgata was heard in the entire world«.

[66] *sarvajña* and *sarvadarśin*. Ch_1: »thanks to his magical wisdom he sees all what is to be seen, without remainder«.

[67] Both Ch. om. this repetition, but we find it in the Khotanese version, stanza 3 (L. p. 7): *biśśu butte sarvañi balysə*, »the omniscient Buddha knows everything«.

[68] *daśabalasamanvāgata*.

[69] *caturvaiśāradyaprāpta*.

[70] *catuḥpratisaṃvitsamanvāgata*.

[71] *aṣṭādaśāveṇikabuddhadharmapratipūrṇa*.

[72] *maitrī* and *karuṇā*. Ch: »neither giving up benevolence nor getting rid of compassion«.

[73] *anāvaraṇabuddhacakṣuḥsamanvāgata*. Ch_1 simply: *fo yen* = *buddhacakṣuḥ*, Ch_2 om.

[74] *pañcacakṣuḥsamanvāgata*. Ch_1 *hui yen* = *prajñācakṣuḥ*, an obvious confusion of *pañca* with *prajñā*, especially of their Middle Indian forms *pañca* and *paññā*.

[75] *prātihārya*. Ch_1: »endowed with the limitless *(wu chi) prātihārya*«.

[76] *ādeśanāprātihārya*, *anuśāsanāprātihārya*, *ṛddhiprātihārya*. Ch_1 begins with *ṛddhiprātihārya*.

For the detailed discussion of all the above features of a Buddha see: Har Dayal, *The Bodhisattva Doctrine*, pp. 19—24, 105—106, 259—267.

[77] Ch_1 om.

[78] Ch_1 om., Ch_2: »grass, trees and forest«.

ocean up to its boundaries[79], the abode of the gods[80], the Horizon-wall[81] and the Trench[82], during an aeon or, at will, still longer.

4. At that time there lived at the great town of Rājagṛha a juggler called Bhadra[83], learned in treatises, skilled in magical spells, profoundly versed in arts and crafts, having completed his magical power[84], skilled in all kinds of performances, very famous and renowned among all the jugglers and the pupils of the jugglers in Magadha[85]. Having converted all the people in Magadha (except the *upāsakas* and the *upāsikās* who saw the Truth and followed the [true] faith and doctrine[86]), having infatuated, bewitched, deceived them with heretical doctrine[87], thanks to the power of his magical and jugglery wisdom[88], he acquired profits, honours and fame.

5. This juggler Bhadra heard that the glory and the laud of the Lord were exalted in verses where he was called the

---

[79] Here the literal translation of T. gives no satisfactory sense and one is obliged to interprete the text freely. Both Ch: »the ocean and the rivers«.

[80] Ch_1: »the palace of gods and *nāgas*«.

[81] *Cakravāḍa*, Ch_2 om.

[82] *Parikhāṭa*, Ch_2 om.

[83] T. *bzaṅ-po* = Ch_1 *po t'o* or (more often) *jen hsien* = Ch_2 *po t'o lo*.

[84] T. *las-kyi mtha'* = *sādhana*.

[85] Ch_1: »and among all the jugglers of Magadha no one could equal him who had [among them] the highest rank«. Ch_2, more briefly: »He was the first among all the jugglers of Magadha«.

[86] Leumann (L. p. 361 f. note 3) asserts that this mention of *upāsaka* and *upāsikā* is missing in Ch_1, in which he is mistaken. This phrase is translated in Ch_1 as follows: »except the *upāsakas* and the *upāsikās* who saw the Truth and attained the *dharmakṣānti*«. *dharmakṣāntiprāpta* replaces here *dharmānusārin* of T. (which is omitted in Ch_2). Leumann's mistake might have been caused by the fact that, in Ch_1, the words *upāsaka* and *upāsikā* are rendered by a rather unusual equivalent *ch'ing ching shih nü*.

[87] T. *ya-mtshan-gyi chos* = *pāṣaṇḍikā dharmāḥ* = Ch_1 *hsieh hsing chih shu*. Ch_2 om.

[88] *māyāvidyabalādhāna*, a heretical countrepart of the 16 *balādhānas* of the Bodhisattva. Ch_2 translates this whole passage in fewer words: »All the unreasonable men were infatuated by the *māyā* and converted to this [heretical] faith.«

Tathāgata, the Arhat, etc.... [89], and it occurred to him: — »All the people of the whole Magadha are converted, infatuated, deceived by my heretical doctrine, and all the brahmins and the householders, as many as there are of them, are delighted with my name. The Tathāgata, the Arhat, the Fully Enlightened One alone was not yet put to the proof, neither infatuated nor deceived [90]. Therefore let me go even now into the presence of the Tathāgata, the Arhat, the Fully Enlightened One, and let me put him to the proof! If I shall be able to infatuate and deceive him, then the whole Magadha will be subdued, and I shall acquire gains, honours and power over the *dharma* [91]«.

6. Thus the juggler Bhadra, driven by the force of his former merits, owing to the magical power [92] of the Buddha, left the great town of Rājagṛha, came to the presence of the Lord, and perceived the Tathāgata emitting a brightness greater than ten millions of suns [93], with a face more immaculate than ten millions of moons [94], with a body stately like the king [of trees] *nyagrodha* [95], with a circle of hair between the eyebrows [96] shining like the effulgence of a stainless jewel, with eyes, the

---

[89] T. repeats here word for word the epithets of § 3. Both Ch. abridge this passage. Ch_1: »The juggler Bhadra heard that the Lord Buddha was praised as the Tathāgata, the Arhat, the Fully Enligtened One.« Ch_2: »The juggler heard that the merits *(guṇa)* of the Tathāgata were praised...«

[90] Both Ch. abridge. Ch_1: »My magic has infatuated all the people of Magadha and this province. The *śramaṇa* Gautama and his disciples are the only people I have not tried to infatuate hitherto.« Ch_2 »All the population of Rājagṛha worships me, the *śramaṇa* Gautama alone is not yet converted.«

The appellation »*śramaṇa* Gautama« befits the unbeliever Bhadra much better than the piling up of titles used in T.

[91] Ch_1 »Let me try whether I shall be able or not to deceive him. If I succeed all the people of Magadha will come to worship me unanimously.« Ch_2: »Now let me go and put him to the proof. If he will be converted, all the people of Magadha will venerate me twice as much.«

[92] *anubhāva.*

[93] Ch_1: »twice as great as [the effulgence of] 10 millions of suns and moons«. Ch_2: »greater than 100 000 suns«.

[94] Ch_1: »the Buddha whose pure and immaculate brightness radiated far away.«

[95] *nyagrodhaparimaṇḍala*, one of the 32 *lakṣaṇas*. Ch_1 om.

[96] *ūrṇākeśa*. Ch_1 gives another of the 32 *lakṣaṇas* : *uṣṇīṣa (chi hsiang)*.

colour of which was like the colour of the opening flowers of the black lotus[97], with the top of his head [too high] to be seen even by Brahma, — and teaching the *dharma*, amidst the assembly, with 8 kinds of voices[98]. And though, having seen such a body and having heard such a teaching, Bhadra was disposed in his mind to believe [in the Buddha], he thought[99]: »Just now let me make a proof in order to be sure whether he is omniscient and all-seeing, or not[100].«

7. Thereupon the juggler Bhadra inclined his head to the feet of the Lord and, in order to put him to the proof, said to him: — »I invite You to dinner for to-morrow[101].« And he thought: »Does he know my intention or does he not? If he knows, he will not come; and if he does not know, then he will

---

[97] Ch_1: »with an effulgence as pure as that of a lotus flower.« Ch_2: »his eyes were of reddish-blue colour like the blue lotus«. It corresponds to the *lakṣaṇa* called *abhinīlapadmanetra*.

[98] Ch_2: »Even Brahma cannot see the top of his head. He was teaching the *dharma* to beings with 60 kinds of pure voices.« Ch_1 is much more laconic: »He was superior to Brahma and taught the *dharma* in details *(vistareṇa)* with 8 kinds of voices«, but this version seems to be the most correct one because it corresponds best to the two following *lakṣaṇas*: *brahmujjugata* (cf. *e. g.* the *Dīgh. Nik.* II, 18) which has no Sanskrit equivalent in the list of Mhv., and *brahmasvara* which contains precisely 8 kinds of voices: *aṣṭāṅgopeta svara.* The number 60 which we find in Ch_2 and in T. is doubtlessly a later reading where *aṣṭāṅgopeta* was replaced by a faulty *ṣaṣṭyaṅgopeta.*

[99] Ch_1: »Bhadra, having seen such a beautiful *rūpakāya*, was very delighted and thought...« Ch_2: »The juggler, though he saw the majesty and splendour of the Tathāgata, continued to be full of false pride and thought...«

Both Ch. om. the theme of the hesitation of Bhadra who, according to T., was almost ready to believe in Buddha. We find this theme in the Khotanese version where Bhadra, having seen the effulgence of the *ūrṇā,* was very much frightened (stanza 57, L. p. 14, 15):

āhu səte rrīysai nāte duṣḍarrau hvāñətə hāḍe
mamə ṣṣadda aysmiya ysāta uho varata kəḍe-buro məstə.

»He shut his lips tightly, held his tongue and said in fright: a great faith in Thee has arisen in my soul.«

[100] Ch_2: »if he is omniscient and all-seeing he must discern my intention.«

[101] Ch_1 shortly: »he invited the Buddha.« Ch_2: »I wish You to accept for to-morrow my humble worship.«

come [102].« The Lord, however, for the purpose of converting the juggler Bhadra and a great part of the inhabitants of the great town of Rājagṛha [103], albeit he was aware of the deceit, accepted, without saying a word, the invitation of the juggler Bhadra for himself and the Order. And Bhadra thought in his heart: »I have the intention to deceive him, and he [104] promised [to come]. Hence he is neither omniscient, nor all-seeing.« And he bent his head to the feet of the Lord [105] and retired.

8. Then the venerable Mahāmaudgalyāyana [106] spoke thus to the Lord: »This juggler Bhadra will deceive the Order with

---

[102] Ch_1: »If he knows my intention he will not accept my invitation; if he does not know, then he will accept it without suspicions.« Ch_2 om. the entire sentence, and it is precisely that sentence which, constituting, so to speak, the essence of the anecdote, appears *mutatis mutandis* in all the variants of this legend, cf. the Pali text (p. 437): *sace sabbaṃ tumhe jānātha mayhaṃ gehaṃ mā pavisatha, mama gehaṃ paviṭṭhānam pi vo n'eva yāgu atthi na bhattâdīni, sace ajānitvā pavisissatha gūthaāvāṭe vo pātetvā pothessāmī.*

In the Khotanese text, see the stanza 51—53 (L. p. 13):

ka viyattu sarvañi īyə ttū butte ṣā ulatāna
ka vā vā tsīyû nai brāte ku mara ātə həmāte
aysvī vā ttīyə hamīhīmə thatau maṃdəru pātcu
kho rro paḍā vəta ulatāna khāysvī ju vaska ne pīpe
tta-ttai pulsīmə ka sarvaṃñu śśāstāro paysāna
cu ne bŭsti ṣā ulatāna c'ū tsutai myāño muḍānu

»If he really be omniscient, he would perceive that this is a cemetery. But if he will come and not notice where he is come, I shall quickly restore the former aspect [of that place] by a spell, it will be a cemetery again and there will be neither drink nor food prepared for him. Then I will ask him: ,If Thou art omniscient and layest claims to the dignity of »the Teacher«, why didst Thou not discern that this is a cemetery, why didst Thou come amongst the dead?'«

[103] Ch_1: »in his care of Bhadra and of the inhabitants of Rājagṛha and wishing to deliver them...« Ch_2: »seeing that the juggler and the inhabitants of Rājagṛha were reaching maturity *(paripakvendriya)* in order to bring about [this ripening] he accepted silently the invitation«.

[104] Ch_1 »*śramaṇa* Gautama«, Ch_2 »Gautama« cf. foot-note 90.

[105] Ch_1 adds: »thrice did the *pradakṣiṇā*«.

[106] Ch_2 adds: »who was in the assembly and saw the whole proceeding.«

his magic[107]«. The Lord replied: »Be not[108] afraid, Maudgalyāyana! I have long ago[109] accomplished the right conduct[110] and, being Tathāgata, I know the proper time[111] [of doing thus]. Therefore the entire world including gods cannot deceive the Tathāgata[112]. Furthermore, Maudgalyāyana, people are infatuated by passion, hatred and delusion[113], but the Tathāgata has[114] completely done away with these defilements and lust[115] and has attained [the recognition] that all the *dharmas* are inexistent from the outset[116]. Therefore, even the entire world including gods cannot deceive the Tathāgata[117].

Furthermore, Maudgalyāyana, the magic of the juggler Bhadra, being incomplete[118], is not the right magic, whereas the magic of the Tathāgata is the right magic, since he has fully realized that the entire reality is but magic[119]. O Maudgalyāyana,

---

[107] Literally: »with the basket *(za-ma-tog = karaṇḍa)* of his magic« *i. e.*, »with the accumulation of his magical powers (?).« But as this »basket« is left untranslated in both Ch., it seems likely enough that here the T. text conceals a misreading; *māyākaraṇḍena* might have been misread for *māyākaraṇena* »performing his magic, by means of magical action.«

Both Ch. are more detailed than T. and add: Ch_1 »Why hast Thou accepted his invitation for Thyself and the Order?«, Ch_2 »Do not accept his invitation.«

[108] I insert here the negation which is missing in all the T. recensions. Ch_1: »be quiet and keep silence!«, Ch_2 »Do not think thus.«

[109] Ch_1 om., Ch_2: »during the long aeons.«

[110] *samyakcaryā*. Ch_1: *p'ing teng hsing = samacaryā*, a misreading which might be best explained as a confusion with the Middle Indian *sammācariyā = samyakcaryā*.

[111] *kālajña*, cf. foot-note 408. Ch_1: »the Tathāgata profoundly discerns the deceits conceived day and night by all the men.« Ch_2 om. this phrase.

[112] Ch_2 om. this phrase. [113] *rāga, dveṣa, moha.*

[114] Ch_2 adds: »long ago.«

[115] Ch_1: »The Tathāgata, as he has cut off passion, infatuation and hatred and completely annihilated fetters like defects and defilements, is free from 80 kinds of defilement.«

[116] *anutpattikadharmakṣānti*. The word *kṣānti* is missing in T. and Ch_2.

[117] Both Ch. add: »and how a man (Ch_1: one little juggler) would be able to deceive me (Ch_1: make a joke of me)?«

[118] T. *phyogs-gcig-pa = ekadeśa* »one-sided, partial.« $Ch_{1,2}$ om.

[119] This phrase is almost entirely missing in Ch_1 where there only remains: »he clearly realizes that all the *dharmas* are but magic and he himself reached Buddhahood.«

if all the beings in the world attached to the nominal reality[120] each possessed as powerful a magic as the juggler Bhadra, even the magic of all of them would reach neither a hundredth, nor a thousandth, nor a 1 000 000 000 000th, nor even an incalculably and incomparably [small] part of the magic of a Tathāgata[121].

9. »How dost thou think, Maudgalyāyana? Could this juggler Bhadra exhibit this Universe containing three thousand thousands of worlds adorned with all their decorations?« — »No« — he replied. The Lord proceeded: — »And the Tathāgata can exhibit, at will, on part of the point of a hair as many adorned worlds as there are grains of sand in the Ganges, and yet it will not be shown by means of the whole magic[122] of Tathāgata.

Maudgalyāyana, the following wind-circles[123] are existing

---

[120] *prajñapti.*

[121] The countreparts of this discourse in the Pali and Khotanese version are the discourses of Buddha with Sirigutta (p. 440—441) and Aniruddha (stanzas 62—77, L. p. 15—17) respectively, though the contents of those discourses present but a very vague likeness. In the Pali text, Sirigutta warns the Buddha that Garahadinna might have treacherous intentions. and the Lord quietens him explaining that he accepted the invitation because he wished to convert all who will be present. In the Khotanese version, Buddha gives a similar answer to the warnings of Aniruddha, but offers a more detailed explanation by means of a digression on the *prātihāryas* as to why he has chosen this way of converting Bhadra, see Introduction, p. 6. This justification of Buddha's way of proceeding which appears in Pali and Khotanese versions is missing in the discourse of Buddha with Mahāmaudgalyāyana (it is however given earlier, see § 7).

[122] Ch.$_2$: *shen li* = *ṛddhibala.*

[123] *vāyumaṇḍala.* In Buddhist cosmology, this term denotes the wind-circle which supports the water-circle *(abmaṇḍala)* on which the entire universe is founded. The *vāyumaṇḍala* in its turn is based on the *ākāśa* (see AK, III, p. 139, *Milindapañha* p. 68, J. Przyluski, JA, 1918, II, p. 418).

The wind-circles, however, enumerated in our text seem rather to correspond to winds which play an important part in the creation and the destruction of successive worlds. The *kalpa* of creation begins with a »primordial wind« *(prāgvāyu)* which aggregates the atoms (AK, III, p. 185). The *kalpa* of destruction *(saṃvartakalpa)* ends with the following stages: the word is burnt by seven suns and the flames driven by the wind spout out till they reach the Brahma world *(tejaḥsaṃvartanī)*; then the water submerges the world and dissolves it like salt *(apsaṃvartanī)*; finally the in the world: »the Scattering Wind« [124] and »the Cutting asunder Wind« [125] which cut asunder the Universe containing three thousand thousands of worlds and destroy it [126]; »the Dispersing and Scattering Wind« [127] which moves in the middle of the world; »the All-Settling Wind« [128] which reaches the top of the world [129]; »the Destroying Wind« [130] which can scatter even Sumeru, the king of mountains, not to mention the common hills [131]; »the Blazing Wind« [132] the flame of which, burning during an aeon, spouts out [133] to the world of Brahma [134]; »the Overcoming Wind« [135] which smothers this fire which burns during an aeon [136];

---

wind scatters and disperses *(vikirati)* the world like a heap of dust *(vāyusaṃvartanī).* See AK, III, p. 184, 185.

Some of the wind-circles enumerated in this § correspond to these cosmological notions. Thus the »All-settling wind« corresponds to *prāgvāyu,* the »Scattering wind« — to *vāyusaṃvartanī,* the »Blazing wind« — to *tejaḥsaṃvartanī* and the »Water-sprinkling wind« — to *apsaṃvartanī.*

[124] T. *rnam-par-'thor-byed = vidhvaṃsana* (?). Ch_1: *sui lan = vairambha.*

[125] T. *yoṅs-su-gcod-byed* = Ch_1 *tuan chieh = paricchedana.*

[126] Ch_2 translates the entire sentence as follows: »the Destroying Wind *(wei sui huai)* which can destroy the *trisāhasralokadhātu,* the *Vairambha (p'i lan p'o)* which can destroy the world and bring it together again. Ch_1 also: »which destroy the world and restore it.«

[127] T. *kun-tu-'thor-byed daṅ rnam-par-'thor-byed* = Ch_1 *chui chu* (?) = Ch_2 *wei ku tung.*

[128] T. *kun-nas-yoṅs-su-'jog-pa* = Ch_1 *chu chih* = Ch_2 *wei an chu.* Ch_1 adds *po li t'u na* which suggests the reconstruction *paridhāna.*

[129] T. *srid-pa'i rtse-mo = bhavakoṭi.* Ch_1: »which reaches the 33 gods.« It is obvious that the reading *san* of the »Yuan« and »Ming« ed. must be substituted to *erh* adopted in Taishō.

[130] T. *rnam-par-'jig-pa* = Ch_1 *ts'ui p'o peng* = Ch_2 *wei p'iao san = vikiraṇa.*

[131] Ch_1 translates only »*Sumeru*«, Ch_2: »*Sumeru,* the king of the mountains, *Kālagiri,* etc.«

[132] T. *'bar-byed* = Ch_2 *wei meng yen = jvalakara* (?). Ch_1 gives *kou na* which is not clear. We find the equivalent of this wind later, see note 137.

[133] In Ch_1 the reading *ch'ao* of the »Three editions«, the »Old Sung« ed. and the »Shōgo-zō MSS« seems better than *ch'i* of Taishō.

[134] Ch_1: »to the heaven of 33 gods.« Here also Taishō reads »32«, see note 129.

[135] T. *rnam-par-sgrub-byed* = Ch_2 *wei chih hsi.* Ch_1 *ch'ang lai* is not clear.

[136] Ch_1: »which, during an aeon, raises the fire on heaven and earth.«

»the Satisfying Wind«[137] which can cover all this Universe containing three thousand thousands of worlds with one cloud[138]; »the Water-sprinkling Wind«[139] which pours out rain during a burning aeon; »the Very Dry Wind«[140] which dries up[141] all that has been damaged by water. O Maudgalyāyana, beginning with the wind-circles I should be able to expound the doctrine during an aeon or still longer, for there are no limits to the teaching of the Tathāgata which begins with the [explanation] of wind-circles«.

»Now, Maudgalyāyana, how dost Thou think? Could the juggler Bhadra remain within those wind-circles?« — »No« — he replied. Then the Lord proceeded: — »And as for myself, Maudgalyāyana, I should be able to keep to all the four kinds of behaviour[142] within all those wind-circles. The Tathāgata can, at will, put all the wind-circles in one mustard-seed, and this seed will not burst. And he can, moreover, show within a mustard-seed all the effects of those wind-circles, and the winds will neither clash nor conflict with one another[143]. Such is, Maudgalyāyana, the essence of my magic[144] which possesses no equal[145] and has no limits[146].«

10. Thereupon the venerable Mahāmaudgalyāyana and the whole assembly bent their heads in admiration to the feet of the

[137] T. *rab-tu-tshim-byed* = Ch_2 *wei ch'ing liang*. Ch_1 *ch'ih huo* corresponds to the »Blazing Wind«, see note 132.

[138] Ch_1: »which causes the entire *trisāhasramahāsāhasralokadhātu* to be consumed by fire in one instant.«

[139] T. *chus-'debs* = Ch_1 *chiao shai* = Ch_2 *wei pien chu*.

[140] T. *lhag-par-skems* = Ch_1 *k'u chieh* = Ch_2 *wei kan chieh*.

[141] Ch_1: »transforms.«

[142] *spyod-lam* = *īryāpatha*. Ch_1 *ssŭ ch'i hsing*, Ch_2 explains what are those 4 kinds of behaviour: »to walk, stand, sit down and lie« and adds: »to remain motionless«.

[143] Ch_1 translates the whole period as follows: »does there exist a man who could remain in the *antarīkṣa* and keep in all the wind-circles the four *īryāpathas*, put all these wind-circles in one mustard-seed so that they did not interfere with one another nor destroy that seed, allowing thus gods and men to remain hidden there in bliss and without fear?«

[144] T. *sgyu-ma'i chos-ñid* = *māyādharmatā*.

[145] Ch_1: »is unsurpassed«, Ch_2 om.

[146] Ch_1 adds: »and neither those who attained the stage *(bhūmi)* of *śrāvaka* or *pratyekabuddha* can equal [this magic].«

Lord and uttered simultaneously the following words: »It is indeed a great gain to us to have a teacher endowed with such a great witchcraft [147], with the glory of such a majesty, with such a great magical power [148]; that is a great gain to us! And whosoever will hear this wonder [149] of the Tathāgata, in him will Faith be born [150], and, as a result of Faith, the thought directed towards Supreme Enlightenment will arise in him. It will be a great gain [151] to him!«

11. In the meantime the juggler Bhadra betook himself to the great town of Rājagṛha [152] and this very night, in that place of the town where rubbish and impurities [153] from the whole city were thrown out, he magically created a great circular courtyard decorated with silk fringes, umbrellas, hoisted banners and flags. On its ground, flat as the palm of the hand, flowers were scattered, aromatic incenses distributed and, right above, a canopy was stretched out. Besides these, he created in that courtyard 8000 gem-trees with flowers and fruits, and, under every gem-tree, he created lion-thrones [154] supplied with many calico-cushions and with a baldachin adorned with gems [155]. On both sides of every lion-throne he created four gem-trees with flowers and fruits [156], and, in order to entertain the Lord and the Order of monks he created dishes flavoured with a hundred various tastes and 500 servants wearing white clothes and adorned with gems.

12. At the very moment the juggler Bhadra had created such an arrangement [157], the Four Great Kings appeared in the shape of huge bodies, came to the courtyard of Bhadra and said: »O Bhadra, Thou hast invited the Tathāgata for dinner

---

[147] *ṛddhi*. [148] *anubhāva*. [149] *prātihārya*.

[150] Ch_1: »he will be delighted.«

[151] Ch_1: »the immeasurable merit.«

[152] Ch_1: »returned to his home.«

[153] Instead of *mi-mthun-pa* appearing in T. which is not clear, one would rather expect *mi-gtsaṅ-ba* »impurities« which is usually found in this combination and which would correspond to Ch.

[154] *siṃhāsana*. Both Ch. add: »for all the monks.«

[155] Ch_1 adds: »and in the middle of the hall he created for the Tathāgata a lion-throne 49 feet high adorned with innumerable gems«.

[156] Ch_2 om. this phrase. [157] T. *bkod-pa* = *vyūha*.

to-morrow and, in order to entertain him, Thou hast created such an arrangement of this courtyard[158]. That is a great gain to Thee[159]. Then, allow us to create a second modest arrangement in order to honour the Tathāgata, to entertain the Lord and to assist Thee!«

Then the juggler Bhadra, struck with amazement, gave his consent to the Four Great Kings, and they created a second arrangement of the same kind[160] in order to entertain the Lord.

13. Thereupon Śakra, the ruler of gods, came with 30 000 gods[161] to the courtyard of Bhadra and said: »O Bhadra, Thou hast invited the Tathāgata for dinner to-morrow and, in order to entertain him, Thou hast created such an arrangement of this courtyard. That is a great gain to Thee[162]. Then, allow us to create a second modest arrangement in order to honour the Tathāgata, to entertain the Lord and to assist Thee!«

Then the juggler Bhadra struck with amazement[163] gave his consent to Śakra, the ruler of gods, and, in order to entertain the Lord, Śakra created a particularly magnificent courtyard such as the *Vaijāyanta*[164], the residence of gods, with the tree *Pārijāta*[165]. The arrangement of the juggler Bhadra and of the Four Great Kings were eclipsed by this last courtyard[166].

14. It then occurred to the juggler Bhadra: »If even such gods as are assembled here strive to worship and to honour the Lord, he must be an extraordinary being, and it does not beseem me to cheat such a high person. It is quite certain that I ought to destroy what I have made[167].« Thus Bhadra tried to withdraw

---

158 Ch_2: »these immeasurable ornaments.»

159 Ch_1 om. this phrase.

160 $Ch_{1,2}$: »which surpassed the arrangement built by Bhadra.«

161 Ch_1: »32 000 gods and men« (the reading *t'ien* of »Yuan« and and »Ming« ed. might rather be substituted to *fu* of Taishō).«

162 Ch_2 om. this phrase.

163 Ch_1 adds: »being overrun with doubt in the depth of his soul.«

164 Not the *Vijaya* tree as Leumann translates (L. p. 363).

165 T. *yoṅs-'du-sa-brtol* = Ch_1 *chih pao shu* = Ch_2 *po li chih to chü ping t'o lo* (= *Pārijāta-kovidāra*).

166 Ch_2 om.

167 Ch_2 abridges: »the juggler, when he saw it, was alarmed and regretted [his deed].«

what he had created, to make it inexistent, to annihilate it and, by means of all spells and charms, to make it invisible, but the food, the servants, the arrangement of the courtyard and the lion-thrones remained visible, as if they were real, and he could not annihilate them by means of all his spells and charms[168]. Then he thought, greatly amazed: »Formerly I could exhibit a magic at will and withdraw it at will; but now, owing to Tathāgata's interference, I cannot make inexistent the arrangement of that place.«

15. Thereupon Śakra, the ruler of gods, having discerned the thought of the juggler Bhadra, said to him: »Bhadra, just as Thou art not able to annihilate the arrangement of this place settled for the sake of the Tathāgata, so, if any man conceives whatever thought directed to the Tathāgata, that thought cannot be withdrawn but will be the inner cause of his [future] *parinirvāṇa*[169]«. Then the juggler Bhadra was pleased, delighted, enraptured, and at the waning of the night, he went to remind the Lord that dinner-time was approaching and asked him: »O Lord when dinner-time will come, be kind enough and remember to condescend to come to my dinner!«

16. Then, at early morning, the Lord put on his undervest and upper robes, took the almsbowl and surrounded by the Order

---

[168] Ch_2 here abridges too: »He wanted to withdraw what he had created by means of spells.«

[169] This allocution of Śakra (for its meaning see foot-note 27) has also a counterpart in the Khotanese version, *viz.* the words of the *devatā* of Rājagṛha which demonstrate to Bhadra (stanzas 82—85, L. p. 19) the greatness of Buddha. The contents of these stanzas have, properly speaking, very little in common with the words of Śakra, but the fact that in both versions there existed such allocutions proves that there might exist a common source for all the versions. Some of the themes of the primitive legend as the discourse of Buddha with the disciple who warns him (see the note 121), the setting up of competitive arrangements by the gods (see the note 22), the presence at Buddha's being put to the proof of two kinds of onlookers: believers and unbelievers (see note 182) etc., — are preserved in different variants in all the versions.

betook himself in front[170] of the monks[171] to the great town of Rājagṛha, to the courtyard of the juggler Bhadra, and performed such a magic that Bhadra had the impression that the Tathāgata was sitting in the arrangement[172] created by him, the Four Great Kings had the impression that the Tathāgata was sitting in the arrangement created by them, and Śakra, the ruler of gods, had the impression that the Tathāgata was sitting in the arrangement created by him[173]. And whoever in Rājagṛha among the heretics[174], the philosophers[175], the wandering mendicants[176], the brahmins[177] and the house-holders[178] heard of that, all of them were greatly astonished and hastened to the courtyard thinking: »Now, let us see how the *śramaṇa* Gautama[179] will be deceived!« And the faithful monks and nuns, the *upāsakas* and the *upāsikās*[180] of the great town Rājagṛha all together hastened to the circular courtyard, thinking: »Now, let us hear the words[181] of the Tathāgata and let us see his great wonder![182]«

---

170 All the T. recensions give *daṅ-la* but it seems very likely that it should be completed: *daṅ-po-la* = »in front«. Both Ch. translate »surrounded« but we find »in front« in the Khotanese version, stanza 78 (L. p. 17): ...*balysə pruhauṣṭe saṃkhālu pāttəru nāte p a ḍ ā pastātə bilsaṃggə* = »The Buddha put on his robe (*saṃghāṭī*), took the almsbowl and walked in front of the Order of monks.«

171 Ch_1: »bodhisattvas, monks and their relatives.« Ch_2: »monks and the people of Rājagṛha.«

172 Ch_1 here and in the following instances: »on the lion-throne.«

173 Ch_2 places the whole of this sentence at the end of the paragraph.

174 T. *gźan-mu-stegs-can* = *anyatīrthika* = Ch_1 *hsieh i tao* = Ch_2 *wai tao.*

175 T. *spyod-pa-pa* = *mīmāṃsaka.* Both Ch. om.

176 T. *kun-tu-rgyu* = *parivrājaka.* Ch_2 *fan chih* = *brahmacarin,* Ch_1 om.

177 Ch_1 om.

178 Both Ch. om. but Ch_1 adds: »having rejected their haughtiness, hatred and anger...«

179 In this place T. translates at last (see the note 90) rightly: »*śramaṇa* Gautama«, but Ch_2 gives: »Tathāgata.«

180 Both Ch. add: »very joyful.«

181 The reading *bgam-pa* of N is the only one which makes sense in T. But taking under consideration the *siṃhanāda* of Ch. (see the subsequent note) it should rather be supposed that there was in T. some »compositum« of *bka'* (cf. the reading *dka' ba* of B and P) meaning »speech, words, precept.«

182 Ch_1: »We shall see the very Buddhahood of the Tathāgata, hear

17. Then the juggler Bhadra, overcoming his pride and arrogance, bent his head to the feet of the Lord and said to him: »O Lord, I confess my great sin in inviting the Tathāgata to come here, with the intention to deceive him. But, [when I realized] that it beseemed not to deceive such a high person by means of magically created food, servants, lion-thrones and courtyard, I wanted to withdraw it. I was however unable to give it up, to revoke it, and even by means of all my spells and charms I could not make it inexistent. The food, the servants, the lion-thrones and the arrangement of the courtyard remained as if they were real[183].«

18. So he said and the Lord spoke thus to the juggler Bhadra: »The enjoyments and gains[184] of all the beings, Bhadra, are created by the magic of the deed[185], this Order of monks is created by the magic of the *Dharma*[186]. I am created by the magic of wisdom[187], the Universe containing three thousand thousands of worlds is created by the magic of all the productions[188]; and the entire reality[189] is created by the magic of the

---

his lion's roar *(siṃhanāda)* and look at his wonders *(prātihārya)*.« Ch$_2$: »They wanted to see the *prātihārya* of the Tathāgata and hear his lion's roar.«

This entire passage agrees almost textually with the corresponding passage in the Pali story (p. 442, 443): *mahājano sannipati, micchādiṭṭhikehi nimantite mahanto sannipāto hoti, micchādiṭṭhikâpi 'samaṇassa Gotamassa vippakāraṃ passissāma' ti sannipatanti, sammādiṭṭhikâpi 'ajja Satthā mahādhammaṃ desessati, Buddhavisayaṃ Buddhalīlhaṃ upadhāressāmā' ti sannipatanti.*

183 Both Ch. abridge this §.

184 *upabhoga* and *paribhoga.*

185 *karmamāyā.* Ch$_1$: »are but *māyā*«.

186 *dharmamāyā.* Ch$_1$: »is but *māyā.*«

187 *jñānamāyā* (and so Ch$_1$ too).

188 T. *mṅon-par-'grub-pa-byed-pa* = *abhiniṣpatti, abhinirvṛtti*, cf. E. Obermiller, *The Sublime Science*, p. 127: »Now, the roots of Phenomenal Existence are the physical and the mental elements *(nāma-rupā)* as they become originated *(abhinirvṛtta* = *mṅon-par-grub-pa)* in the (3) spheres of this world«.

Ch$_1$: »by the *māyā* of the causes and conditions such as sins and merits« (the full stop has to be placed 4 characters further than in the Taishō ed.). Ch$_2$: »by the *māyā* of all the beings together.«

189 *sarve dharmāḥ.*

complex of conditions[190]. But now, Bhadra, as Thou knowest that the time has come, give us the meat, the drink and dainties to taste and to suck that Thou hast created.« And the Lord and the Order of monks consumed the food for eating, drinking, tasting and sucking that had been magically created by the juggler Bhadra with his magical servants, by the Four Great Kings and by Śakra, the ruler of gods[191].

19. On that occasion[192] the *sthavira* Mahākāśyapa uttered this verse[193]:

»Just as[194] is the gift, so[195] is the receiver. If one penetrates into the profound nature[196] [of both], the offering may become perfectly pure.«

20. Mahāmaudgalyāyana said:

»The arrangements for sitting[197] and those who sit on them, do not differ[198]. And, since they are identical, this offering is pure and unsurpassed.«

---

[190] *pratyayasaṃbhara*. For this entire declaration of Buddha cf. St. Schayer, *Vorarbeiten zur Geschichte der mahāyānistischen Erlösungslehren*, Zeitschr. für Buddhismus, 1921, p. 53, 54.

[191] Ch_2: *Brahmarāja*.

[192] The stanzas which follow present some sort of incantations purifying Bhadra's offering by showing that the real value of this offering consists in the understanding that, just as this gift is illusory, so are also the givers and receivers and the entire reality (see also § 76). The gift of Bhadra, though it was offered with treacherous intentions, becomes purified by the fact of Budhha's accepting it (see § 67 and note 337).

As to the method of translation of these gāthās see p. 13.

[193] In Ch_1 stanza 19 is omitted and the subsequent stanza is put in Mahākāśyapa's mouth.

[194] In Ch_2, in stanzas 19 and 20, *ju* may be substituted to *chih*$_1$. The sense is clearer in Ch_2 than in T.: »just as the gift (the food) is but magically created, so is the receiver. If we know that both are identical, the *dāna* may be called pure«.

[195] Both the meaning and the Ch. texts prove that we have here: »just as... so...« and not »just as... just as...« as in T. The same is true of the following stanzas.

[196] *dharmatā*, in this case: »their identity.«

[197] Ch_2: »just as seats are but magically created...«

[198] In Ch_2 the second half of this stanza is identical with the second half of the preceding stanza. Ch_1: »when we know that [both] are identical, this *dāna* becomes the best and unsurpassed.«

21. Śāriputra said:
»Just as is the mind of the worshipper, and just as is the mind of the receiver, so is the giver too. Hence the offering may quickly become pure [199].«

22. Subhūti said:
»[Since one bestowed] offerings here, giving nothing in reality, and since they were received by those who, in reality, do not receive, — all those who came here offered a pure gift [200].«

23. Ānanda said:
»This is a gift of Space [201]. It was received by inconceivable [202] [receivers]. They who are delivered from mind and body [203] are themselves the supreme offering!« [204]

24. The Bodhisattva Prabhāketu said:
»Just as the juggler Bhadra magically created this arrangement [205], so [illusory] is the entire reality. Only fools do not conceive that.«

25. The Bodhisattva Prabhāvyūha said:
»Just as all these seats and trees are but magically created, so [is all] void like the magic of the mind [206]. There exists no difference in this respect [207].«

26. The Bodhisattva Siṃha said:
»The jackals scream in the jungle until they do not hear the lion's roar. But as soon as they become aware of that roar they flee in panic in all directions [208].

---

[199] Ch_1: »Thus their identity is to be conceived. Then the offering is unsurpassed and pure (*hsin* may be based on a false reading *śraddha* instead of *śuddha*).

[200] Ch_1: »they all ought to do it because it is the highest and the purest (here also *hsin* for *śuddha*) *dāna*.« Ch_2 repeats the ending of stanza 21.

[201] *ākāśadāna*. Ch_2: »this is a gift like *ākāśa*.« Ch_1: »Such a gift is the most honourable *(tsun)* vehicle *(ch'eng = yāna)* [leading to Salvation].«

[202] Ch_2 *pu k'o te* = »unseizable.« [203] *cetokāyavimukta*.

[204] Ch_1: »are in the world the protectors of beings.«

[205] *vyūha*. Ch_1: »displayed this magical manifestation.«

[206] *manomāyā*.

[207] $Ch_{1, 2}$: »is there any difference between the *manomāyā* and the *śūnyatā*?« A literary translation from T. affords no satisfactory sense.

[208] »in 10 directions«. Ch_2: »they flee and hide themselves [nobody] knows where«.

27. Similarly[209] the juggler Bhadra, so long as he had not been seen by the Tathāgata[210], [boasted] among the heretics, proclaiming: »I am greater than the Victorious One!«
28. O Bhadra! The magic of the Tathāgata demonstrates what [real] magic is. If one took [this magic] as the measure of the teaching, even Māra would not be able to fathom its depth[211].«
29. The Bodhisattva Siṃhamati said:
»These meats are magically created, these servants are also magically created and those who enjoy them are magically created too! This is the meritorious and unsurpassed offering[212].«
30. The Bodhisattva Maitreya said:
»Just as fire increases gradually as ghee[213] and sesame-

---

209 Ch_1 om. stanza 27.

210 Ch_2: »so long as he had not found himself in the presence of the Tathāgata.«

211 Ch_1: »O venerable Bhadra! Your [power] is limited (the reading *hen* of Taishō should be replaced by *hsien* attested in the »Three editions« and the »Old Sung ed.«), albeit by Your *māyā* You can deceive men. But the *māyā* which Tathāgata displays cannot be [fathomed] even by many Māras.« Ch_2: »Albeit the juggler may create [illusional reality], his *māyā* is limited whereas the *māyā* produced by the Tathāgata has no limits. Even all the gods and Māras cannot know its boundaries.«

A reflection of the §§ 26–28 may be found in the Khotanese version in the following words of Aniruddha (stanzas 64,65 L. p. 15):

...trāmu tvī vaska hăṃgrīta ulatāñe harbiśśə thərtha
kho ju sarvai vaska pharāka rrūvâsa cā'yyō Badrə
tvī hiviyo bvāmato balysa ggumācē yande gyaḍīna

»Thus for Thy sake all the heretics met on the cemetery just as the eaters of the [lion's] crumbs (*rrūvâsa* = skt, *lopāśa* »jackals) [assemble] near the lion. In his foolishness Bhadra [wants] that Thy knowledge, o Buddha, be fathom.d (*ggumace yande*) by means of his magic (*cā'yə* = *māyā*).«

212 The translation of Ch_2 constitutes for us a kind of commentary to this stanza: »If a n y b o d y k n o w s that this gift, these meats and those who enjoy them are but *māyā*, [this knowledge] is a meritorious and unsurpassed gift.«

213 Ch_2 has in Taishō su_1 = *soma* which should be replaced by su_2 = *sarpiḥ* attested in »Yuan« and »Ming« editions. This confusion is frequent, Cf. R. p. 94 foot-note 214.

oil are poured over it, so, owing to the magic of Bhadra, the magic of Buddha becomes manifest[214].«

31. Manjuśrī, the prince royal, said:
»Just as all this is undone[215] from the outset, so the whole reality is always equally [unreal] from the very beginning.«

32. Then, with the purpose of converting the juggler Bhadra, the Lord created a householder who came[216] to the courtyard and said to Bhadra: »What are You doing, Bhadra?« — »I am entertaining the *śramaṇa* Gautama[217] to dinner.« — he replied. The householder said: »Let it alone, Bhadra, do not say it! Now, the Tathāgata, together with the Order of monks, is taking his meal at the king Ajātaśatru's palace.« And the juggler Bhadra saw indeed, owing to the magical power of Buddha[218], the Tathāgata together with the Order of monks taking their meal at the king Ajātaśatru's palace.

Then the Lord created a second householder who came to the courtyard and said to Bhadra: »What are You doing, Bhadra?« — »I am entertaining the *śramaṇa* Gautama to dinner.« — he replied. The householder said: »Let it alone Bhadra, do not say it! The Tathāgata with the Order of monks is gone on the road of the religious mendicants[219] to gather alms.« And the juggler Bhadra saw indeed, owing to the magical power of Buddha, the Tathāgata together with the Order of monks gathering alms on the road of the religious mendicants.

---

214 Ch_2: »This is what happens with Buddha's *māyā* by the *māyā* of Bhadra.«

215 *akriya*. Both Ch. translate this stanza in greater details. Ch_1: »Just as this place is magically created from the outset by the spells of Bhadra by means of which he deceives men, so are all the *dharmas* equally [unreal] from the outset. Those fools who have not understood it are involved in the *saṃsāra*.« Ch_2: »Just as this assembly and these good things were not existing (lit. »made«) before, so all the *dharmas* are equal from the beginning and eternally.«

216 In Ch_1 the reading *lai* of the »Shōgo-zō MSS.« should be adopted in the place of *tung* of Taishō.

217 Ch_1 adds: »and the *bhikṣusaṃgha*.«

218 *buddhānubhāvena*.

219 T. *kun-tu-rgyu* = *parivrājaka*. Ch_1: *i tao* = heretics, Ch_2: *fan chih* = *brahmacarin*.

Then the Lord created another householder who came to the courtyard and said to Bhadra: »What are You doing, Bhadra?« — »I am entertaining the *śramaṇa* Gautama to dinner.« — he replied. The householder said: »Let it alone, Bhadra, do not say it! The Tathāgata now preaches the Truth in the pleasure-grove of Jīvaka [220] to the fourfold assembly [221].« And the juggler Bhadra saw indeed, owing to the magical power of Buddha, the Tathāgata preaching the Truth in the pleasure-grove of Jīvaka to the fourfold assembly.

Then Śakra, the ruler of gods approached the juggler Bhadra and said: »What are You doing, Bhadra?« — »I am entertaining the *śramaṇa* Gautama to dinner.« — he replied. Śakra said: »Let it alone, Bhadra, do not say it! The Tathāgata preaches now the Truth to the Thirty Three gods in their abode, under the *Pārijāta* tree [222]. And the juggler Bhadra really saw the Tathāgata preaching the Truth in the abode of the Thirty Three under the *Pārijāta* tree.

33. He perceived the Body of the Tathāgata adorned with the marks (of Mahāpuruṣa) and surrounded by monks, on every leaf and on every flower of all the trees magically created by him; he perceived the Tathāgata surrounded by the monks also on every lion-throne both on those which he himself had magically created and on those which the Four Great Kings had conjured up [223]; and he saw the body of the Tathāgata, adorned with marks on all the walls, houses, palaces, streets and ways as many as there were of them in Rājagṛha. And before all these Tathāgatas, Arhats and Fully Enlightened Ones he perceived himself, with his head bent to earth, confessing his sin, and he saw nothing else but Tathāgata in the range of his vision. He became then enraptured, delighted, overjoyed, thanks to this satisfaction he attained the *buddhānusmṛti-samādhi* [224] and, as soon as

[220] $Ch_{1,2}$ add: »king of physicians.«

[221] *bhikṣus, bhikṣuṇīs, upāsakas* and *upāsikās*.

[222] Ch_1 adds: »day and night«, Ch_2 om.: »under the *Pārijāta*-tree.«

[223] Ch_1: »...on those which the Four Great Kings and Śakra Brahmarāja had magically created...«, Ch_2 om.

[224] So both Ch. In T. *dad-pa-rjes-su-dran-pa'i tiṅ-ṅe-'dzin* corresponds to *śraddhānusmṛtisamādhi*, probably a false reading *śraddhā°* for *buddhā°*.

he rose from that trance, he sat down near the Lord and holding forth clasped hands uttered these verses[225]:

34. »I became convinced[226] of the magical power[227] of the Tathāgata who, at will, creates many Buddhas, more than 100 000, as many as there are grains of sand in the river Ganges.
35. I thought before that in Jambudvipa nobody equaled me for training and level of magic[228]. But to-day, when I saw the magical power of the Victorious One, [I realized that I] cannot equal his [power] even in number, in its [smallest] part.
36. All those whom I saw with my bodily eye had their bodies adorned with the marks of the Victorious One[229]. Now, I beseech the King of Truth: »tell me who is the real Victorious One?«
37. Let the All-seeing[230] tell me which of them I ought to worship[231] and who will acquire the merit for it? And who will attain the corresponding Enlightenment?[232]
38. Now, I confess here my sin of putting the Ruler of the World[233] to the proof. Beings which do not prac-

---

[225] These gāthās offer great difficulties since T. has very often an irregular syntax and, when translating them, one should rather go by the sense deducted from all the three versions. In Ch_1, in the Taishō ed., the division of verses is wrong: each stanza should consist of 8 quadrisyllables and not of 6.

[226] T. *mos-(pa)* = *adhimukta*. Ch_1: »I saw the magical power...«, Ch_2 interchanges stanzas 34 and 35 and translates § 34 as follows: »I understand from it that the inconceivable power of the Buddha allows him to create magically, at will, as many Buddhas as there is sand in the Ganges.«

[227] *ṛddhi*. [228] *māyābhūmi* (?). T. is not clear.

[229] Ch_1: »I saw nothing else but the Buddhas adorned with marks...«

[230] T. *kun-tu-spyan* = *samantacakṣuḥ* = Ch_1 *p'ing teng p'u chien*, Ch_2 om.

[231] Ch_1 »Who should be venerated first, on whom should the *dāna* be bestowed?«

[232] Ch_1 has, instead of *bodhi*, *ch'ing ching* = *śuddhi* (?), cf. foot-note 243. Ch_2 abridges: »I wish to worship [one] of those Tathāgatas. Let the Lord deign to instruct me as to who is the most dignified one«

[233] *lokanātha*. Ch_1: »the Great Hero *(mahāvīra)* and Teacher.« Ch_2 adds: »...and I make the vow to attain the *parinirvāṇa*.«

tise devotion to the Highest Being[234], spoil the work of bliss performed by the Victorious One[235].

39. O Gods, Śakra and Brahma[236], and all who are assembled here, listen to me![237] The thought of Enlightenment will arise in me with the purpose of delivering all creatures.

40. I treat all beings with an entertainment, and I will satisfy them with the delight of nectar[238]. Let creatures obscured by sleep be awakened by him who attained the splendour[329] of transcendental wisdom[240].

41. Is it possible that in him who sees[241] such magical transformations, who has heard the ravishing words of the Sugata, and [come to know] his intelligence free from attachments[242] and his excellent conduct — the thought directed on Enlightenment[243] should not arise?

42. Please explain me which is the Path of Enlightenment, practised by the knowers of Enlightenment[244].

---

234 *sattvavara.*

235 Ch_1: »they abandon themselves and do not fulfil their wishes.« In Ch_2 the translation of this part which precedes the first sentence of stanza 38 sounds: »If any one has no devotion *(bhakti)* to Buddha, such a man *(pṛthagjana)* looses his bliss.«

236 Ch_1 om. 237 Ch_2: »be witnesses!«

238 T. *bdud-rtsi* = *amṛta* = $Ch_{1,2}$ *kan lu.* In Ch_1 *yin* has to be changed into *wen* and *an wen* = *yogakṣema* »uttermost peace« would correspond to *bde-ba* of T. Ch_2 interchanges the sentences.

239 T. *mthu* = *tejas* = Ch_1 *teng ming* = Ch_2 *kuang ming.*

240 *prajñā.* Ch_1: »let the creatures obscured by sleep attain the splendour of the finest *(viśiṣṭa)* wisdom.« Ch_2: »and let the worldly beings *(shih men* = *loka, laukika)* be awakened by means of the splendour of *prajñā.*«

241 Ch_1: »creates.«

242 *asaṅga jñāna.* Both Ch. link these two words and it is far better than in T. where *chags-pa-med-pa* = *asaṅga* is connected with *spyod*=*caryā.*

243 Here also I follow Ch_1 *tao i* = Ch_2 *p'u t'i hsin*=*bodhicitta.* In T. *dag-pa* may result from a false reading *śuddhi* instead of *bodhi* (cf. footnote 232). In Ch_1 the interrogative character of this stanza is not distinctly indicated.

244 Ch_1: »I beg Thee to explain me the most perfect *(nipuṇa) bodhimārga* and [to tell] which Venerable One ought I to serve in order to attain the *buddhamārga*?«. Ch_2: »I beg Thee to explain me the *bodhimārga* and the purest conduct.«

Which is their conduct with which the conduct of the *śrāvakas* cannot be compared? [245]

43. What are the merits of observing the rites? [246] What should be the devotion [247] of those who wish to hear the teaching? What must be the conduct of the amiable [248] [bodhisattvas]? Tell it me, so that I should have no doubts [249].

44. What may be the application to the search of learning? [250] And what is the beginning of fixing in the mind what one has heard? And how does one teach others, how can beings attached to life [251] believe in the doctrine? [252]

45. How can those men neglect the reward for their teaching and remain disinterested? [253] How do they become grateful, useful and inseparable friends [254] of beings?

46. To which friends may one adhere, and how must one avoid bad friends? [255] What is the way to meet the Buddhas, and, having seen them, how must one worship them? [256]

---

[245] Ch_2: »What is the conduct which cannot be attained by the two vehicles (= the *śrāvakas* and the *pratyekabuddhas*)?«

[246] T. *cho-ga* = *vidhi*. Ch_1: »...of practising the unconditioned *(asaṃskṛta)* [elements] (?).« Ch_2: »what is the conduct?«

[247] Ch_1: »the right doctrine *(sadartha)*«, Ch_2: »what is the devotion of a *peśala (tsun chung*, cf. the following foot-note).

[248] T. *des-pa* = *peśala*. Ch_1 om., Ch_2 cf. the preceding note.

[249] Ch_1: »How can the absence of doubts arise?«, Ch_2: »with what behaviour *(īryāpatha)* are endowed those who have no doubts?«

[250] Literally: »of hearing«. Ch_1: »What is the energy *(vīrya)* of insatiably *(atṛptam)* hearing?« Ch_2: »what may be the insatiability of hearing?«

[251] In Ch_2 *ling* should be replaced by *ming*.

[252] Ch_1: »Of what kind is the light by means of which *dharma* enlightens men?«

[253] T. *zaṅ-ziṅ-med-pa'i sems* = *nirāmiṣacitta*.

[254] So Ch_2 T. om. In Ch_1 the whole stanza differs entirely: »What is the way of offering which produces affection *(maitrī)* and makes one's heart inseparable [from others]? What are the offerings which can satiate all mankind and make firm their affection?«

[255] Ch_2 »evil thoughts.«

[256] Ch_2: »to adore tirelessly.«

[257] *śikṣā*.

47. What is the pure training[257] and devotion?[258] And how can one master this training?[259] How does conduct become perfectly pure?[260] And how can one reach the perfectly pure concentration?[261]

48. How must one practise what is right and reject what is not right?[262] How does the well determined will[263] make one who is in trouble unseizable for the Māra's snares[264].

49. And how does a faithful one meditating upon the true sense not forget the beings in his mind? How can he who brings beings to maturity[265] remain firm[266] in avoiding to collect wealth.

50. How can a man enter into the right conduct[267] and find a support in the ressources[268], benevolence[269] and compassion?[270] How can those who have purified their consciousness[271] and thoughts[272] fully develop supernatural faculties?[273].

---

[258] *bhakti*. Ch_1: »What training should be applied in order to attain the highest rank?«

[259] Ch_1: »wisdom«. [260] Ch_2 om. this phrase.

[261] T. *tiṅ-'dziṅ* = *samādhi*. Ch_2: »Which conditions (*gotra*, see footnote 481) of concentration produce the regular (*yoniśaḥ*) mentality?«

[262] Literally: »how must one be *saṃprayukta* with what is *yoniśaḥ* and *viprayukta* from what is *ayoniśaḥ* ?« Ch_2 interchanges these expressions. Ch_1: »How can one fulfil the pure conduct and reject the *adharma* ?«

[263] T. *śin-tu-ṅes-par bsam-yid* = *suniścita āśaya*.

[264] Ch_1: »How can those who are weak in spirit subdue the Māra who wishes to ensnare them?«, Ch_2: »How those who are not weak, cannot be caught by Māra?«

[265] Ch_2: »does not forsake beings.«

[266] I follow here Ch_1 which gives *chien ku* = *dhīra*. It is more suitable than T. The T. translator may have read *vīra* = *dpa'-ba* which is a very frequent confusion, cf. R. p. 71 foot-note 84. Ch_2 om.

[267] Ch_1: »the conduct consisting in not forsaking men.«

[268] T. *thabs* = *upāya* = Ch_2 *fang pien*. Ch_1 om. All the T. recensions write wrongly *thams*.

[269] *maitrī*. [270] *karuṇā*. [271] *smṛti*.

[272] *mati*. Ch_2 om. this phrase, Ch_1: »and what is the *mati* and the will (*chih*$_2$ = *kratu* replaces here *nien* = *smṛti*) of an eminent Bodhisattva (*tao hsin* ?)

[273] *abhijñā*.

51. How does a man who is endowed with comprehension [274], spells [275], acquiescences [276], who does not divert from his vow [277] and pure conduct, who is the knower of the profound doctrine and the highest Truth, — how does he fulfil all his vows?

52. How do those who reached Perfection [278], attain the corresponding Enlightenment? He who knows the behaviour of a Bodhisattva, for Enlightenment's sake will not deviate from that conduct [279].

53. O Thou omniscient, knower of the right doctrine [280], ocean of wisdom, source of knowledge [281], tell me all those things! O Lord, explain me those advantages [282], I wish so earnestly to fix it all in my heart!«

54. Thereupon the Lord uttered these verses to the juggler Bhadra:

»He who is able to create magically all the *dharmas*, creates ten thousand millions of Buddhas who appear in millions of magically created lands [283] and lead there to deliverance millions of beings.

55. Just as Thou, Bhadra, createst out of something immaterial [284] the manifestation of innumerable and various material objects [285] which are neither originated, nor disappearing, which are without past, future or present [286],

---

[274] *pratisaṃvid.* [275] *dhāraṇī.* [276] *kṣānti.*

[277] *praṇidhāna.* Both Ch. translate *pratibhāna.* It is obvious that there occurs a confusion between these words which resemble each other. The context (»...does not divert from...«) points out that rather the T. translator has read correctly. The author of Ch_2 seems to have misunderstood the 2nd and the 3rd *pada* which he translates: »One must reject the *dharmas* which have to be rejected in order to penetrate into the profound doctrine.«

[278] *pāramitā.*

[279] Ch_2: »Those who reached Perfection do not deviate from what they have attained.«

[280] *sadarthajña.* [281] Ch_2 om. all these epithets.

[282] T. *phan-yon* = *ānuśaṃsa.* $Ch_{1,2}$: »O merciful Lord, explain me that!« Both Ch. om. *ānuśaṃsa* and add »merciful«. Could it be a confusion of *ānuśaṃsa* and *anukampa(ka)*?

[283] *kṣetra.* [284] *arūpa.* [285] *rūpa.*

[286] *anutpanna, aniruddha, agata, anāgata, apratyutpanna.*

56. so the »Man-Bull«[287], the Victorious One creates the psychophysical elements of his own [personality][288] and the Order of monks which are neither originated, nor disappearing.[289] Such is the magical power of the inconceivable Buddhas[290].

57. Just as men deceived by magic are seing with their obscured mind elephants, horses, chariots and foot-soldiers[291] which in reality were neither created[292] nor have left any trace[293],

58. so the Buddhas [must be considered] as immaterial[294], colourless[295] and formless[296], having no conduct[297] nor behaviour[298]. One may not inspire the conviction that real personalities exist[299], and one may not consider that Buddha is really a Buddha[300].

59. The Buddha cannot be conceived through its material aspect[301], nor signs[302], neither through his age and lineage[303], nor through his voice[304]. His mind cannot be explained[305] and [his nature] cannot be analyzed by the consciousness.

---

287 *nara-puṅgava.* 288 *skandhāḥ.*

289 So Ch_2 which adds: »and reaching the *nirvāṇa.*« Ch_1: »which are without future and without duration (*hou* must probably be substituted to *ts'ung*)«. T. means: »they do not become *ajñāna* (probably a false reading for *ajāta*)«.

290 Ch_2: »the inconceivable magical power of the Buddhas.«

291 *hasty-aśva-ratha-patti-kāya*, so $Ch_{1, 2}$. T. seems corrupt again and instead of this gives: »They are unconscious and free from pride (?).« I do not know how to explain this version. 292 *asiddha.*

293 Ch_1: »there sits and there walks nobody«, Ch_2: »this army is deprived of self-existence (*asvabhāva*) and origin.«

294 *arūpa.* 295 *avarṇa.* 296 *asaṃsthāna.* 297 *caryā.*

298 *īryāpatha.* Ch_2 translates this *pada:* »without past and future.«

299 *satkāyadṛṣṭi.* $Ch_{1, 2}$ seem to have read *matkāyadṛṣṭi.*

300 Ch_1: »though he is awakened (*buddha*) he is not a Buddha; such ideas must be given up.« Ch_2: »There arises a false notion of Buddha.«

301 *rūpa.*

302 *nimitta.* In a correct syntax *mtshan* should precede *mi-lta* just as in the following line *sgra* should precede *ma-yin.* 303 *gotra.*

304 Ch_1: »the voice with which he teaches«, Ch_2 *fan yin sheng* = *brahmasvara*, cf. the subsequent note.

305 This *pada* is missing in both Ch. It is possible that we have here a later T. emendation: formerly in the place of *'chad-par* »to explain« there

60. The Lords Buddhas who are the Ultimate Reality[306] are beyond the three [empirical] Times[307] and their marks do not exist[308]. They are eternally delivered from the essence of illusion[309], and their *dharmas* cannot be calculated[310].

61. The Buddhas who appear [in the world] do not appear really[311]. The aggregates[312] and the components[313] of their [individual personality] do not exist[314]. The basis[315], of these *dharmas* is motionless[316], it cannot provide any support[317], and affords no foundation even for the fivefold sight[318].

---

could be *tshaṅ(s)-par* which would correspond to *brahma°* missing in the actual T. translation of *brahmasvara*. As the syntax of this stanza is very awkward, it is not unlikely that *brahma-* was put in that place, but it made the text quite impossible to unterstand for later copists who therefore introduced the emendation *'chad-par*.

[306] *dharmatā*.

[307] *trikālaśūnya* »devoid of past, present and future«. Ch_2: »surpassing the three Times«.

[308] literally: »do not arise«. Ch_2: »their proper nature is without marks.«

[309] *māyāsvabhāva*, omitted by both Ch. Ch_1: »They are unborn and purified from the outset *(ādiśuddha)* from erroneous views *(dṛṣṭi)* (?). Ch_2 om. the entire sentence.

[310] T. *bgraṅ-bar rab-tu-phye-ba-med* = *gaṇâprabhāvita* = literally: »cannot be analyzed by means of numbers«. In T. this *pada* has two syllables outside the metre. N. restores the right number of syllables by omitting *chos-su* but this is the most important word of the sentence, attested in both Ch. and it cannot be removed. Ch_1 translates: »They have no *dharmas* but their merits *(guṇa)* are good.« We have probably here a confusion of *gaṇâprabhāvita* with *guṇaprabhāvita*.

[311] *dharmatânutpanna*. Ch_2 *svabhāvenânutpanna*, Ch_1 om. this phrase instead of which it gives: »[The Buddhas] are pure from the outset *(ādiśuddha)* and incalculable.«

[312] *skandha*. [313] *dhātu*.

[314] Ch_1: »they have neither the 4 material elements *(mahābhūta)* nor any covering of psychophysical components [of their personality] *(yin kai* = *skandhâvaraṇa*. *yin*$_1$ = *skandha* attested in the »Ming. ed.« should be substituted to the reading *yin*$_2$ of Taishō).«

[315] *pratiṣṭhā*.

[316] *acala*, it means: »free from the *spandana* not manifesting itself (see Schayer, OLZ, col. 407)«. Ch_2 om.

[317] *anālaṃbya*.

[318] *pañcacakṣuḥ*. Ch_2: »the *dharmakāya* of Buddha cannot be seen

62. If any one thinks: »I have seen the Buddha«, he has not really seen the Buddha. The invisible Guide is seen as the trace of [the flight] of a bird in the sky[319].

63. O Bhadra, know that those several Buddhas that thou hast seen, are all one and the same[320]. Myself and anybody else are all alike, just as everything seems alike to us when we look into the skies[321].

64. [Virtue[322]] and contemplation[323] are equal, intelligence[324] is equal, deliverance[325] is equal, the perfect intuition of deliverance[326], and the powers[327] — all those features of the Victorious One[328] are equal[329].

65. They are equal from the point of view of emptiness[330], and all are grounded in the Ultimate Reality[331] free

---

by the fivefold sight.« Ch_1: »it (=*pratiṣṭhā*) cannot be conceived even by the sight of wisdom (*prajñācakṣuḥ*, see note 74).«

[319] Ch_1: »If he sees what cannot be seen, it means that he sees the Guide (*nāyaka*). It is as if he tried to grasp the sky by raising his hand.«

[320] *ekârtha*. Ch_2 om.

[321] Ch_1 om. this comparison but adds: »they all (the Buddhas) have the right wisdom (*samyagjñāna*) and the same marks.« Ch_2: »they are identical as the skies, possess but one mark (= are *ekalakṣaṇa*) and are undifferentiated.«

[322] *śīla*, missing in T. but attested in both Ch. Cf. also note 326.

[323] *samādhi*. [324] *prajñā*. [325] *vimukti*.

[326] *vimuktijñānadarśana*. We have here the so-called *asamasamāḥ skandhāḥ* of the Mhv. IV called also *anāsravaskandhāḥ* (AK, VI, 297 note 2): *śīla, samādhi, prajñā, vimukti* and *vimuktijñānadarśana*. They correspond to the *dhammakkhandhas* of the Pali Canon (see *Dīgha-Nik.* III, 229, 279, *Itivuttaka*, 104 etc.). It is why I followed Ch. in keeping *śīla* in spite of T. (see note 322). On the contrary *bala* which follows does not belong to this scheme.

[327] Ch_2 om.

[328] *jinaguṇa*. The aforesaid elements are also called *jinaskandhas* (see AK, VI, p. 297, note 2).

[329] Ch_1 translates the last *pada* as follows: »all these powers are names for the features of the Buddha«

[330] T. literally means: »are equal as they are grounded on the point of view of *śūnyatā*.« Ch_1: »They are equal in the sense of emptiness (*śūnyatârthena*) and follow the *mārga* (or the *bodhi* = *tao*).« Ch_2: »They are all grounded in the *śūnyatā*.«

[331] *dharmatā*.

from any attachment. They all, being delivered from the essence of illusion[332], are unoriginated[333].

66. Having worshipped one of the Victorious Ones, Bhadra, thou worshippest the Buddhas of the entire Universe[334]. Such is their and my own Absolute Nature[335] in which no plurality can be found[336].

67. All [the Buddhas] purify the gifts by accepting them[337]. And all the offerings will deserve a great reward[338]. All these [Buddhas] participate in the same and perfectly pure Ultimate Reality[339]. As far as Buddhas are concerned there is no [real] plurality[340].

68. Let us now examine who is the real Victorious One[341]. Plunged in earnest meditation[342] with the mind concentrated on one point[343], pondering over and analyzing the ways of the *dharma*[344], listen to me with a properly focussed mind[345]!

69. All[346] they, Bhadra, are unborn and unreal; only those

---

332 *māyāsvabhāva.*

333 Ch_1: »They all are like illusion *(māyā)* [being in reality] pure and delivered from the outset, there is nothing to be accomplished, all what arises [is in reality] perfectly pure.« Ch_2 »They all are like illusion without essence *(asvabhāva)* and origin *(anutpanna).*«

334 literally: »the Buddhas of ten directions *(diś).*« Ch_2: »many Buddhas.«

335 *dharmadhātu.* Ch_1: »all the *dharmas* are identical«, Ch_2: »the *dharmakāyas* of the Buddhas are identical and without difference.«

336 Ch_2 om. this phrase to which the expression »without difference« (see the preceding note) corresponds, and adds: »thus all the Buddhas can provide happiness and profit.«

337 Ch_1: »They can purify the gifts offered by men with faith.« Ch_2 om. Cf. foot-note 192.

338 *mahāphala.* 339 *dharmatā.*

340 $Ch_{1,2}$ add: »... nor difference.«

341 Ch_2: »Thou hast asked me before who is the real Buddha.«

342 *smṛtyupasthāna.* 343 *ekāgracitta.*

344 T. *chos-tshul = dharmanaya.*

345 *suniścitena cittena.* Both Ch. abridge this stanza. Ch_2: »Give up these erroneous *(viparīta)* thoughts and listen to my explanation! Practise the *smṛtyupasthāna* and examine all the *dharmas.*« Ch_1: »On a wrong way *(viparīta)* thou willst not see the Buddha. Now let the features of all the Buddhas be investigated without remainder and without difference.«

346 Ch_1 om. the whole stanza in the place of which it inserts § 71.

who err [think that] they see all this[347]. If things[348] had a reality in the absolute aspect[349], they could not disappear in any respects[350].

70. Therefore[351] they[352] are unborn, unreal[353], and, being unborn, they are not liable to disappearing[354]. Consequently they are invisible and, if it seems that they have any reality[355], after deeper consideration they appear to be without foundation[356].

71. Just as Bhadra sees the Victorious One, just as here around are seen the magically evoked objects[357], so the 5 *skandhas* to which so many fools[358] adhere should be considered in the same manner.

72. All the *dharmas* are without proper essence[359], and the beeings who do not possess the marks of Buddha and wish to acquire the mark of having no marks[360] are distant from the Buddha[361].

---

347 Ch$_2$: »All this is unborn and only those who err see it as real.«

348 *bhāva*. Ch$_2$ *se hsiang* = *rūpalakṣaṇa*.

349 Ch$_2$: »if they were born.«

350 In Ch$_2$ the reading *i* of Taishō should be replaced by *wu* attested in the »Three editions« and the »Old Sung« ed.

351 In Ch$_1$ § 70 comes after § 71.

352 Ch$_2$: »the Tathāgatas«. 353 Ch$_2$ om. »unreal«.

354 Ch$_1$: »being placeless (*wu ch'u* = *aniketa*) are unfixed (*wu so li* = *apratiṣṭhita* ?).« Cf. R. foot-notes 162 and 166.

355 Ch$_1$: »they are invisible and have no material appearance.«

356 Ch$_2$ translates the whole sentence as follows: »when deeply contemplating the Tathāgata [one realizes that] one is seeing what is not visible.«

357 Ch$_1$: »Just as thou, Bhadra, seest the Buddha and just as are objects magically created by thee...,« Ch$_2$: »Just as thou seest the Buddha who does not lean upon all which is here around...«

358 I follow here Ch. Ch$_2$ has *fan fu* = *pṛthagjana*, Ch$_1$ *yü ch'ih* = *bāla*. The T. *stobs* is simply a misreading *bala* for *bāla*.

359 *asvabhāva*. Ch$_1$: »These five *skandhas* are like the *māyā*.«

360 *ekalakṣaṇa* means *alakṣaṇa*, see R. p. 90, foot-note 190.

361 In Ch$_2$ the translation of this stanza is not clear: »the Buddhas and the *dharmas* which reach among the beings (?) have the mark of having no marks and are not based on anything. They who thus conceive them will speedily attain Enlightenment.« The translator has probably read *adūra* instead of *dūra*: »they are not far from Buddhahood.« This reading however, seems more logical than the versions of T. and Ch$_1$.

73. Know that all the *dharmas* are non-existent and [seemingly] arise only thanks to mental constructions[362]. They are unsubstantial[363] and conditioned by causes[364], they are undone and beyond every doer and are qualified as »void« only in order to give them a name[365].
74. He who understands that conditions and efficient causes[366] do not exist[367], knows also that the *dharmas* are freed from passion[368]. And having conceived the *dharmas* free from passion he contemplates the Buddha[369] with a perfectly pure eye.
75. After this teaching had been recited in verses, the juggler Bhadra easily attained the insight of the *dharma*[370] and obedience to Truth[371], within 5000 beeings the thought of Supreme Enlightenment, a thought which they had never conceived before[372], arose and 200 Bodhisattvas attained the acceptance of the doctrine that all the *dharmas* are without origination[373].

---

[362] T. *kun-tu-rtogs-pa* = *saṃkalpa* = Ch_1 *hsiang ch'u* = Ch_2 *wang fen pieh.*

[363] *abhāva*, Ch_1: *wu hsing chih shu* which is very strange, and I cannot explain this term. Would it be a rendering of *adravya* based on a wrong etymology (from *dravya* »wooden«)?

[364] *pratītyasamutpanna.*

[365] T. *miṅ-du-'dzin-pas* = *saṃjñāgrāheṇa.* Ch_1: »when considering the doer and the plurality they are beyond any perception (*saṃjñāgrāha*, we find here this expression, but it is interpreted in a different way than in T.) and inexistent from the outset (*pen wu* = *ādyabhava* or perhaps *ādiśūnya*).« Ch_2: »being *pratītyasamutpanna* they are void, for their essence is beyond any doer.« The implication *pratītyasamutpanna* > *śūnya* is current in early Mahāyāna but it is not an equation, see de La Vallée Poussin, Mel. Chin. Boudh., III, 1935, p. 380.

[366] *hetu* and *kāraṇahetu.*

[367] Ch_1: »He who knows the conditions and efficient causes...,« Ch_2: »he who knows that conditions and efficient causes are void...«

[368] *vītarāga.* Ch_2: »...knows that the *dharmas* are free from passion and pure.« [369] Ch_1: »*bodhi (tao)*« instead of »Buddha«.

[370] T. *chos-la ṅes-par-rtog-pa* = *dharmanidhyapti.* Both Ch. om.

[371] *ānulomikī kṣānti* and not *dharmānusāriṇī kṣānti* as Leumann translates, L. p. 364. This is the second of the three principal *kṣāntis.* For its meaning see Suzuki, *Studies in the Laṅkāvatāra Sūtra*, pp. 126—127 and Har Dayal, *The Bodhisattva Doctrine*, p. 213.

[372] Ch_2 om. this sentence.

[373] *anutpattikadharmakṣānti.* Ch_1: »200 gods and men acquired the

Then the Lord, after having consumed the magical dishes, in order to purify[374] the gift of the juggler Bhadra, uttered the following stanza:

76. Since he who gives and he to whom it is given and the gift itself do not differ[375], all the offerings are equal. Then let this gift become fully meritorious[376] for Bhadra!

77. Then the venerable Ānanda[377] thus spoke to the Lord: »O Lord, I ask Thee to cause by means of Thy sustaining power[378] this adorned courtyard to last for seven days and not to cease existing.« Thus he spoke and the Lord caused by means of his sustaining power this adorned courtyard not to cease during seven days and to look as if it really existed. After this the Lord got up from his seat and went away with the Order of monks.

78. And when the Lord arose from inner concentration[379], sat down on Vulture's Peak hill[380] in order to teach the doctrine, and the monks, the Bodhisattvas, the gods, the *nāgas*, the *yakṣas* and the *gandharvas*[381] assembled around him to hear his teaching, the juggler Bhadra came to the presence of the Lord, bent his head to his feet, walked round him three times, stretched forth his clasped hands with reverence and respect, sat down near the Lord and thus spoke: — »O Lord, explain me the Path of the Bodhisattvas who, following this Path, strive to attain the highest essence of Enlightenment[382].« And the Lord answered thus to the juggler Bhadra: — »Listen then, Bhadra, and pay attention to what I shall tell thee.« — »All right« — Bhadra answered and listened to the Lord who then spoke:

---

purity of the *dharmacakṣuḥ* which became quite free from impurities and defilements.«

374 Ch_1 »in order to make it meritorious . .«, Ch_2: »in order to make it full (*paripūraṇāya*, this reading seems the best, see stanza 76).« By identifying the giver and the receiver who are both illusional and thus making all offerings equal, Buddha endows with merit Bhadra's spurious offering. Here again we have a kind of incantation.

375 Ch_1: »He who offers without thinking of the reward attains purity.«

376 *paripūrṇa*. 377 Ch_1 Mahāmaudgalyāyana. 378 *adhiṣṭhāna*.

379 $Ch_{1,2}$ om. 380 So Ch_2. Ch_1 and T. om.

381 Ch_1: *chien t'a ho* (in the Shōgo-zo MSS. The reading of the other MSS. is faulty). 382 *bodhimaṇḍa*.

79. — »There are, Bhadra[383], four Paths of the Bodhisattvas which lead those who follow them to the highest essence of Enlightenment. And what are these four? 1. not to reject the thought directed on omniscience[384], 2. not to forsake beings, 3. to be insatiable in searching after the root of merits[385] and 4. to develop energy in carefully watching over the Highest Truth[386]. These are, Bhadra, the four Paths of the Bodhisattvas which lead those who follow them to the highest essence of Enlightenment.

80. There are, Bhadra, four [kinds] of perfectly pure conduct[387] of the Bodhisattvas. What are these four? 1. perfectly pure threefold[388] discipline[389], 2. perfectly pure intention[390], 3. perfectly pure knowledge and 4. perfectly pure rebirth[391]. These are the four [kinds of conduct].

81. There are, Bhadra, four *dharmas* inaccessible to the *śrāvakas* and *pratyekabuddhas*[392]. What are these four? 1. transgression of the lower trances[393], 2. an analytical mind[394], 3. great

---

383 Ch_2 adds: *shan nan tzŭ* = *kulaputra* (and similarly in the subsequent §§). This appellation which replaces the denomination »juggler« as the sign of Bhadra's being considered to be already one of the confraternity, does not appear in T. and Ch_1 before § 131.

384 Ch_1: »always to develop the thought directed to omniscience«, Ch_2: »never reject the *bodhicitta*.«

385 T. and Ch_2: *kuśalamūla*, Ch_1: *guṇa*.

386 *paramadharma*. Ch_1 = *sarve dharmāḥ*.

387 *pariśuddhā caryā*. Ch_1 adds: »leading to the highest essence of Enlightenment *(bodhimaṇḍa)*. 388 $Ch_{1,2}$ om.

389 *trividha saṃvara* which consisits in: 1. the restraint according to the *Prātimokṣa (prātimokṣasaṃvara)* which belongs to the *kāmadhātu*, 2. the restraint produced by the *dhyāna (dhyānaja saṃvara)* which belongs to the *rūpadhātu* and 3. the undefiled restraint *(anāsrava saṃvara)* which belongs to the Path and corresponds to pure morality (see AK, IV, p. 43, for other classifications of *saṃvaras* cf. *Visuddhimaga* I, p. 7 and the Commentary on *Dhammasaṅgani*, p. 351).

390 *āśaya*. T. *gnas* is based on a faulty reading *āśraya*. Besides, *āśraya* and *āśaya* not only resemble each other in sound but possess also a doctrinal connection (see AK, IV, p. 24).

391 *upapatti*. 392 Ch_2: »to the two Vehicles.«

393 *dhyāna*. Ch_1: »to transcend the four *dhyānas*,« Ch_2: »not to follow the *jāti (sheng* ?) when practising the *dhyānas* ?« Here probably the reaching of higher states of concentration *samāpattis* is recommended.

394 *cittapravicaya*. Ch_2: »mind analyzing the profound sense.«

compassion towards beings and 4. ability in discussion[395] and multiplicity of arguments[396]. These are the four *[dharmas]*.

82. There are, Bhadra, four noble behaviours[397] of the Bodhisattvas. What are these four? 1. to abide in solitary places, 2. to avoid wordly bustle[398], 3. to feel affection toward beings found in that [solitary] place[399] and 4. to know that all conditioned elements[400] [of reality] come from nowhere and go nowhere[401]. These are the four [noble behaviours].

83. These foundations[402], Bhadra, of deference and esteem towards the Bodhisattvas endowed with four *dharmas* should be mentioned[403]. What are these four? 1. [the Bodhisattvas] are indifferent towards life and body[404], 2. they are always joyful in spirit, 3. they are free from conceit and haughtiness and 4. they fulfil what they say they will do[405]. These are the four [foundations].

84. The following, Bhadra, are the perfections[406] of behaviour[407] of the Bodhisattvas endowed with four *dharmas*. What are these four? 1. knowledge of proper time[408], 2. moderation[409], 3. loneliness[410] and 4. righteousness[411]. These are the four....

85. The following, Bhadra, are the indubitablenesses of the Bodhisattvas endowed with four *dharmas*. What are these four?

---

[395] *pratibhāna.*

[396] literally: »the diversity of words.« Ch_2: »the *pratisaṃvid (wu ai)* of explaining the *dharma*.«

[397] *āryāś caryāḥ.* Both Ch_2: *īryāpatha.*

[398] to be *avakṛṣṭa.* Ch_1 links points 2 and 3 into one (the second) point.

[399] T. *gnas = vihāra.* Ch_1 has *hsing*, which also translates *vihāra* but rather in the meaning of »mode of living« and, consequently, it means: »beings which follow such a mode of living.« Ch_2 om.

[400] *saṃskārāḥ.*

[401] See *Bodhicaryāvatāra*, IX, 142, AK, V, 59 and *Saṃyukta Āgama* XIII, 22. Ch_1 translates points 3 and 4 as follows: »(3) not to have recourse to adulation and untruthful conduct and (4) to aim at the *bodhicaryā* (?).«

[402] T. *gnas*, both Ch. om.

[403] Ch_1 is not clear, Ch_2: »there are four kinds of esteem.«

[404] *kāyajīvite 'naveksinaḥ.* [405] Ch_1: »they carry out orders.«

[406] *saṃpatti.* [407] *īryāpatha*

[408] *kālajñāna*: »to know the proper time for anything.«

[409] *mātrajñāna.* Ch_1: »teaching in a way that gives people pleasure.«

[410] Ch_1: »bashfulness *(hrepana ?)*.«

[411] *samyaktvam.* Ch_1: *chih tsu = śamatha* (?).

1. to dispell repentance[412], 2. to show respect towards learned men and those possessed of great knowledge, 3. to ponder over the meaning of what one has heard[413] and 4. even if anyone when talking does not say the correct things, out of kindness[414] not to point to his mistakes. These are....

86. These four advantages[415] of the Bodhisattvas, Bhadra, when perceived by anybody, make him strive to know[416] them. What are these four? 1. to accumulate one's own and other people's wisdom, 2. to cut short doubts coming from all sides[417], 3. to watch over the Highest Truth[418] and 4. te be inexhaustible[419] in glorifying the Buddha. These are....

87. The following, Bhadra, are the four essential characters[420] of the profoundly learned[421] Bodhisattvas. What are these four? 1. having learnt[422], to know the *dharmas*[423] in details[424], — that is [the first] essence[425], 2. having learnt, not to do what should not be done, — that is [the second] essence, 3. having learnt, to explain it to others, — that is [the third] essence and 4. having learnt, [to understand] the truth[426] that deliverance consists in turning towards Enlightenment [such as was reached by] the Lords Buddhas, — that is the [4th] essence.

88. There are, Bhadra, for the Bodhisattvas four advantages of teaching the doctrine. What are these four? 1. they receive food after work, 2. they are supplied with robes, alms, bedding, medical attendance and medicinal appliances[427], 3. they can weaken the power of their adversaries[428] and 4. they follow gods desirous

---

412 *kaukṛtyaṃ vinodayati*, cf. *e. g. Aṅguttara Nik.* V, 72. Ch_2: »to defend oneself against remorses«, Ch_1 differs entirely: »to teach men with deference (?).«

413 Ch_1 »not to go into the rights and wrongs of the teaching of others.«

414 *maitrī*. 415 *ānuśaṃsa*.

416 literally: »to hear.« Ch_2: »there are four [kinds] of insatiability of the *bahuśrutas*.«

417 Ch_1 »to answer questions and doubts.«

418 *paramadharma*. 419 *akṣaya*. 420 *sāra*.

421 *bahuśruta*. 422 literally: »having heard.«

423 Ch_2: »the *paramadharma*«. 424 *viśeṣena*.

425 *sāra*. Ch_1: *kuei* = *śarana*, Ch_2 om. 426 *artha*.

427 Ch_2 abridges: »robes, medicine and various services.«

428 literally: »of the opposite party.« $Ch_{1,2}$: »of Māra with his attendants.« Ch_1 links points 2 and 3 into one point.

of the *dharma*, and, owing to the protection of these gods, Māra cannot get the opportunity[429] [to do them any harm]. These are, Bhadra, for the Bodhisattvas the four advantages of teaching the doctrine.

89. The following ways of speaking[430], Bhadra, should be used by the Bodhisattvas endowed with four *dharmas* and explaining the doctrine to others[431]. What are these four? 1. to be unostentatious[432], 2. to be contented[433], 3. to have a good and gentle[434] character and 4. to fulfil [the precepts] of their own religion. These are, Bhadra, the four [ways of speaking].

90. There are four *dharmas*, Bhadra, which, possessed by the Bodhisattvas make them avoid the gains obtained by knowledge and render them disinterested teachers of the doctrine[435]. What are these four? 1. they root up[436] the fear of the *saṃsāra*, 2. they do not take care of wordly goods and affairs[437], 3. they watch over others and 4. they lean upon the noble lineage[438]. These are, Bhadra, the four *[dharmas]*.

91. The Bodhisattvas, Bhadra, who are endowed with four *dharmas* are grateful[439], thankful[440] and are useful in return [for what they have received themselves[441]]. What are these four? 1. to compel others to strive towards Enlightenment, 2. not to squander [the good dispositions acquired by former] deeds[442],

---

[429] *nâvatāraṃ labhate*. Ch_1 om. this passage but adds as the fourth point: »he does not show disrespect to others (?).«

[430] *vacanapatha*.

[431] Ch_1: »[the ways] of attaining the power of illuminating the assembly.«

[432] *alpeccha*. [433] *saṃtuṣṭa*. [434] Ch_2: »gentle in speech.«

[435] *nirāmiṣadharmadeśaka*. In Ch_1 *wu i* corresponds to *nirāmiṣa*. Would it be a misreading: *nirviśeṣa*?

[436] I translate here according to the Ch. versions. T. in all the recensions gives *(b)skyed-pa*. The confusion might have arisen in T. tradition (the resemblance of *skyed* and *skrod)* or it might be a misreading *samudgata* instead of *samudghāṭa*.

[437] Ch_1: »the profits of wordly honours.« Ch_2: »wordly goods and friends.«

[438] *gotra*. For the meaning of that term in the Mahāyāna see E. Obermiller, *The Sublime Science*, Acta Orientalia, IX, pp. 99–111. Ch_1 instead of *gotra* has *tao yüan* = *bodhipraṇidhāna* (?).

[439] *kṛtajñā*. [440] *kṛtavedin*.

[441] Ch_1: »...retribution for good and evil.«

[442] *karman*. Ch_1 *kung* = *guṇa* (?).

3. to love one's neighbour as oneself and 4. to make use of the skillfulness of a saint[443] These are, Bhadra, the four *[dharmas]*.

92. The Bodhisattvas, Bhadra, who are endowed with four *dharmas* become the inseparable friends of beings. What are these four? 1. to be equipped with the armour of the force of forbearance[444], 2. not to hope even for a slight profit[445], 3. not to reject the Great Compassion and 4 not to abandon those who rush into error[446]. These are, Bhadra, the four *dharmas* which make the Bodhisattvas inseparable friends of beings.

93. The Bodhisattvas, Bhadra, should adhere to four friends. What are these four? 1. the perfection[447] of *yoga*[448], 2. the perfection of intention[449], 3. the perfection of conduct[450] and 4. to advise Enlightenment to everybody[451]. These are the four [friends].

94. One should learn to know[452], Bhadra, the four bad friends of the Bodhisattvas. What are these four? 1. to teach [the doctrine of] the Small Vehicle[453], 2. to divert anybody from the desire of Enlightenment[454], 3. having acquired adherents (?)[455], to multiply [with their help] the bad *dharma* and 4. to destroy the work of good *dharmas*. These are....

95. The Bodhisattvas, Bhadra, who are endowed with the following four *dharmas* shall meet the Lords Buddhas. What are

---

443 *satpuruṣa*, Ch_2: *bodhisattva*.

444 *kṣāntibala*, Ch_2: *kṣāntipāramitā*.

445 Ch_2 adds: »from beings.« Ch_1: »not to tempt other people and their family (?).«

446 Ch_1: »to aim at delivering and leading towards the Path people who are determined by bad or good conditions,« Ch_2: »not to renounce even in spite of persecution *(viheṭhana)*.«

447 *saṃpad*, Ch_1 om.

448 Ch_1: *ho*$_1$ *ho*$_2$ = *saṃyoga* (the reading of the »Ming ed.« and the »Shōgo-zō MSS« is better than *ho*$_2$ *ho*$_1$ of Taishō), Ch_2 *upāyakauśalya*.

449 *āśaya*. Ch_2 = *viśiṣṭa āśaya*, Ch_1: »to be yielding (?).«

450 *caryā*. Ch_2: »the right conduct of a Bodhisattva.«

451 Ch_1: »to approach Enlightenment gradually.« Would it be a confusion of *upadeśayati* with *upagamayati*?

452 Ch_2: »one should avoid...«; this is probably the best reading. It is possible that we have here a confusion of *prahātavya* with *prajñātavya*.

453 Ch_2: »of the two Vehicles.«

454 Ch_1: »to advise people to destroy the *bodhisattvamārga*.«

455 Ch_2 om. this passage which, besides, is not clear in T. and Ch_1

these four? 1. concentrated mindfulness[456], 2. proclaiming the glory of the Lords Buddhas again and again[457], 3. perfectly pure virtue[458] and 4. pronouncing the vow with full decision[459]. These are...

96. Seeing the following four advantages, Bhadra, the Bodhisattvas will feel delight in worshipping[460] the Tathāgata. What are these four? 1. they will worship the highest dispenser of gifts[461], 2. having worshipped me[462], they will cause other beings also to worship me, 3. having worshipped[463] the Tathāgata, they will make firm[464] their thought directed on Enlightenment and 4. having seen personally[465] [the Tathagata], supplied with 32 marks of the Mahāpuruṣa, they will hoard up a stock of merits[466]. Seeing these four advantages, Bhadra, the Bodhisattvas will feel delight in worshipping the Tathāgata.

97. Thus, Bhadra, the Bodhisattvas having seen the four purposes[467], will apply themselves to training[468]. What are these four? 1. to go beyond the realm of misery[469], 2. to attain[470] the realm of bliss[471], 3. to worship the Tathagata and 4. to fulfil their vow. These are the four [purposes].

98. The following, Bhadra, are the four trainings[472] of the Bodhisattvas. What are these four? 1. not to give up the thought

---

[456] *ekāgrasmṛti.* Ch_2: »the mindful calling of attention on Buddha (*ekāgracittabuddhāvadhāraṇa*).«

[457] $Ch_{1,2}$: »to praise the good qualities (*guṇa*) of the Buddha.«

[458] *pariśuddha śīla.* Ch_2: »the acquiring of perfectly pure restraint (*pariśuddhasaṃvarasamādāna*).«

[459] *adhyāśayena.* Ch_1: »to have the intention (*āśaya*) not to renounce the vow.«

[460] $Ch_{1,2}$: »...are not lazy in careful worshipping...«

[461] Ch_1: »protector,« Ch_2: »when worshipping me, they become an unsurpassed field of merits (*anuttara puṇyakṣetra*)«; that means that through this worship they are planting the seeds of their future reward.

[462] I follow here Ch_2. T. has: »having seen me.« It is possible that here *mthoṅ-nas* is but a mistake for *mchod-nas*. but cf. Ch_1 which means: »having s e e n me they (or others) will follow [my ?] example.«

[463] Ch_1 here again: »having seen...«

[464] *dhruva.* [465] *pratyakṣeṇa*, both Ch. om. [466] *kuśalamūla.*

[467] *arthavaśa.* [468] *śikṣā.* [469] *durgati.*

[470] In Ch_1 of course the reading *kuan* (»to travel with pleasure«) of the »Old Sung ed.« should be substituted to *ch'üan* of the other MSS.

[471] *sugati.* [472] *śikṣā.*

of Enlightenment, 2. to be equanimous towards all the beings[473], 3. to aim at the Highest Perfections[474] and 4. not to be terrified when hearing that the *dharmas* of the Budhda[475] are immeasurable and equal[476]. These are, Bhadra, the four trainings of the Bodhisattvas.

99. The following, Bhadra, are the four perfectly pure trainings of the Bodhisattvas. What are these four? 1. not to do what should not be done[477], 2. to believe in emptiness[478], 3. not to reject the Enlightenment of the Buddha[479] and 4. rightly to suppress the dormant bias to wrong views[480]. These are, Bhadra, the perfectly pure trainings of the Bodhisattvas.

100. The following, Bhadra, are the four conditions of concentration[481] for the Bodhisattvas. What are these four? 1. to avoid wordly bustle[482], 2. to [seek] solitude[483], 3. [to have] an untroubled spirit and 4. to rely upon the store of one's own merits[484]. These are, Bhadra, the four conditions of concentration.

101. The following, Bhadra, are the four [things] which rightly[485] may be practised by the Bodhisattvas. What are these four? 1. having acquired the store of merits to conceive[486] the

---

473 *sarvasattvasamacitta*, cf. Mhv. 833. T. seems to have omitted *sems.*

474 *pāramitās.* 475 Ch_2 om.: »of the Buddha.«

476 Both Ch. om.: »equal.«

477 Ch_1: »to do what is good,« Ch_2: »not to do evil.« 478 *śunyatā.*

479 Ch_1: »not to commit sin through wrong views *(mithyādṛṣṭi,* cf. note 480) being suspicious«. Ch_2: »not to slander the Buddha«, it seems to be the normal Chinese equivalent of the expression *buddha-(bodhiṃ) pratikṣipati,* see R. p. 93, foot-note 211.

480 *dṛṣṭyanuśaya.* Ch_1: »to be free from doubts,« Ch_2: »to suppress the *dṛṣṭis.*«

481 *samādhigotra.* For the use of *gotra* as a synonym of *hetu* (or *bīja)* see AK, VII, 49.

482 to be *avakṛṣṭa.*

483 Ch_1 leaves this point untranslated and puts instead the following sentence: »to have the soul pure and free from attachments« which corresponds to the 3rd point.

484 *kuśalamūla.* Ch_2: »to increase the *kuśalamūla*«, Ch_1: »to fulfil the *kuśalamūla*« (this being in Ch_1 the 3rd point, the following sentence, as point 4, is added: »to approach gradually the *bodhi* of Buddha«).

485 *yoniśaḥ.*

486 *sākṣātkurvanti.* Ch_2: »they turn to the *bodhicitta*«, Ch_1 abridges the first point: »to produce the store of merits«.

thought of Enlightenment, 2. to have no hindrance for inner concentration[487], 3. to be acquainted with the doors of deliverance[488] and 4. not to enter into predestination[489]. These are, Bhadra, the four things....

102. There are, Bhadra, four wrong mental dispositions[490] which have to be rejected. What are these four? 1. to be frightened by the dread of *saṃsāra*, 2. not to trust ascetics[491], 3. not to delight[492] in the hidden meaning[493] [of the teaching] and 4. not to produce the store of merits[494]. There are, Bhadra, four....

103. The following, Bhadra, are the four resolutions[495] of the Bodhisattvas. What are these four? 1. »even for one[496] being's sake may I attain deliverance aeons[497] later and may I walk round the orb of transmigration many aeons longer!« — this is the first resolution, 2. »may I know the mental attitudes[498] of all the beings in order to calm their defiling troubles[499] and may I teach the doctrine in order that others should become

---

487 *samāpattyāvaraṇa.*

488 *vimukter āyadvāra*, see AK, I, p. 48.

489 *niyāma*, probably *samyaktvaniyāmāvakrānti* is concerned *i. e.* the entering into the predestination of attaining the *samyaktva* which here is a synonym of *nirvāṇa*, see AK, VI, p. 80. A Bodhisattva in contrast to the Śrāvaka does not aim at personal *nirvāṇa* and therefore does not seek the *[samyaktva]-niyāma*. This interpretation is corroborated by Ch_2 which does not constitute so much a translation as a sort of commentary: »not to aim at the *nirvāṇa* of the two Vehicles.« Ch_1 is not clear.

490 *ayoniśaś cittotpāda.*

491 *yogācāra*. Ch_1: »to seek deliverance in the *kuśalamūla*« which here is not suitable.

492 Ch_2: »not to believe in... (*sheng chieh* means here *adhimukta*).

493 *saṃdhi*. For the recent discussion of the meaning of *saṃdhi* see E. Lamotte, *Saṃdhinirmocana*, p. 12 f., J. R. Ware, JAOS, 57. 122 and F. Edgerton, JAOS, 57. 185.

494 Ch_1 is not clear.

495 *ceto(vi)niścaya*. Ch_2: »right intentions (*samyaksaṃkalpa*)«, Ch_1: *chiang fu ch'i hsin*, probably an abstr. of *nimna* or *ninata* (*chiang fu* = »bent on, inclining to, aiming at«) meaning »aim, purpose,« cf. *e. g.* the Pali *ninnatattā* (Commentary on *Dhammasaṅgani*, 39 and Stede's *Pali Dictionnary*, s. v. *ninnata*).

496 T.: »for a few beings' sake.«

497 Ch_1: »10 000 *koṭis* [of *kalpas*]«, Ch_2: »innumerable *kalpas*.«

498 *cittacaryā*. 499 *kleśa*.

acquainted with the highest Lord above whom there is no higher[500]!« — this is the second resolution, 3. »may I reject all the unfavourable[501] *dharmas* and, being supplied with all favourable *dharmas*, and leaning on the highest essence of Enlightenment[502], may I defeat the army of Māra and attain Supreme Enlightenment!« — this is the third resolution, 4. »may I teach the doctrine explaining in one word[503] the entire Universe containing three thousand thousands of worlds[504]!« — this is the fourth resolution. These are, Bhadra, the four resolutions....

104. The following, Bhadra, are the four *dharmas* enabling one to subdue Māra[505]. What are these four? 1. to contemplate[506] the *dharmas* as being illusional[507], 2. to practise the regular knowledge[508], 3. not to consider all the *dharmas* as different[509] and 4. not to rely upon all signs[510]. These are, Bhadra,....

105. The following, Bhadra, are for the Bodhisattvas the four meditations[511] over the truth. What are these four? 1. since the *dharmas* are not individual[512], they are dependently originated[513] and no *dharma* arises without cause[514], 2. the *dharmas*

---

500 Ch_1: »...and let me teach the doctrine according to a former vow«, Ch_2: »let me know the different sensuous natures of beings and let me teach the doctrine [to beings] in order to remove their defiling troubles.«

501 *akuśala.*

502 *bodhimaṇḍa.* Ch_2 om. the passage concerning the *bodhimaṇḍa.*

503 T. *ekasvareṇa.* Ch_1 om. *eka°*, Ch_2: *ekabrahmasvareṇa.*

504 Ch_2: adds: »and innumerable beings.«

505 Ch_2: »the intrepidities which cannot be broken by Māra.«

506 *pratyava* + *ikṣ-*, cf. AK, VII, p. 3 foot-note 2.

507 *māyā iva.* Ch_1 adds: »and pure.«

508 *yoniśo jñāna.* T. om. *jñāna*, Ch_1 differs entirely: »to attain the *anutpattikadharmakṣānti.*

509 Ch_1: »[to understand] that differentiation is ignorance.«

510 *nimitta.* Ch_1 differs: »to transcend the *saṃsāra* and practise the right conduct.«

511 *cintanā.* 512 *apudgala*, both Ch. om. this passage.

513 *pratītyasamutpanna.*

514 Ch_2 divides the 1st point into two points which are translated as follows: »(1) to know that all the *dharmas* are *pratītyasamutpanna* and (2) to know that there is not even a slight *dharma* which does not arise as conditioned *(wei = saṃskṛta ?).*«

110. The Bodhisattvas, Bhadra, endowed with four *dharmas* should possess skilfulness in the choice of means[536] [for converting others]. What are these four? 1. one should know that all the thoughts[537], even sinful ones, not to mention meritorious thoughts, lead towards the thought of Enlightenment[538], 2. one should view all the beings[539] as vessels[540] of the *dharma*, 3. having understood that the *dharmas* are devoid of proper nature[541], one should realize that they may be considered as real only by mistake[542], and 4. those who are desirous of deliverance should cultivate inner concentration[543] and cognizance[544] free from clinging to anything[545]. The Bodhisattvas, Bhadra,....

111. The following four affections, Bhadra, have to be cultivated by the Bodhisattvas. What are these four? 1. the cultivation of affection[546] [expressed in the words]: »let me be the refuge[547] of all the beings[548]«, 2. the cultivation of affection [expressed in the words]: »let me lead all the beings to deliverance«[549], 3. the cultivation of affection [expressed in the words]: »let me remind to all the beings [their aims][550] and 4. the cultivation of affection [expressed in the words]: »let me lead all the beings to the *parinirvāṇa*[551]«. These four affections, Bhadra,....

112. There are, Bhadra, four compassions[552] of the Bodhi-

---

536 *upāyakauśalya.* Ch_1 places § 110 after § 112.

537 *cittotpāda.* In Ch_1 the older reading might have been *chü* (attested in the »Old Sung ed.« and the »Shōgo-zō MSS«) instead of *hsiang* of Taishō *hsin chü* represented probably *cittapada*, a misreading for *cittotpāda*.

538 See Introduction, p. 8. The theory of *upāyakauśalya* regards a certain amount of trickery and falsehood as permissible, see Har Dayal, *The Bodhisattva Doctrine*, p. 251. In Ch_1 the words: »even the sinful ones, not to mention meritorious thoughts« constitute the 2nd point.

539 Both Ch. add: »beings clinging to wrong views *(mithyādṛṣṭi)*.«

540 *bhājana.* 541 *asvabhāva.*

542 Ch_2 abridges: »one should consider all the *dharmas* as *asvabhāva.*« Ch_1, where it constitutes the 2nd point, differs: »one should consider all the *dharmas* as *buddhadharmas*, as having reached the *samyaksaṃbodhi.*«

543 *samāpatti.* 544 *saṃjñā.* 545 Ch_1 om. this point.

546 *maitrībhāvanā.* 547 *śaraṇa.* 548 Ch_1 »illusional beings.«

549 *tārayitavyam.* In Ch_1 it constitutes the 3rd point.

550 *smārayitavyam.* Ch_1 seems to translate it (in point 2) as follows: »let me lead beings to the attainment of the *dharma.*«

551 Ch_1: *wu wei* = *asaṃskṛta.* 552 *karuṇā.*

sattvas. What are these four? 1. the compassion consisting in transfering beeings from the realm of misery[553] into the realm of bliss[554], 2. the compassion consisting in inducing the beings who cultivate sinful deeds to adopt the good religion, 3. the compassion consisting in inducing beings professing [the doctrine of] the Small Vehicle to embrace the way of the Great Vehicle and 4. the compassion consisting in leading all the beings to the *parinirvāṇa*[555] These are the four [compassions].

113. By the Bodhisattvas, Bhadra, endowed with four *dharmas* the following supernatural faculties[556] are attained. What are these four? 1. lightness[557] of body and mind[558], 2. a thorough insight of the universal Illusion[559], 3. an attitude of reverence and devotion towards all the beings[560] and 4. [the possibility] of remaining completely undisturbed[561], being absorbed in quiescence[562].

114. By the Bodhisattvas, Bhadra, endowed with four *dharmas* the following comprehensions[563] are attained. What are these four? 1. to rely on the meaning[564] and not on the letter[565], 2. to rely on the teaching[566] and not on the man, 3. [to know] that the grammatical meaning[567] of all the *dharmas* has no proper

---

[553] *durgati.*

[554] *sugati.* Ch_1: »to be the friend of those who are in the *durgati* and lead them to the *sugati.*«

[555] Ch_1: »to cause all the beings to be joined by compassion.« Ch_2: »to cause all the beings to get out of the *saṃsāra* and attain the *nirvāṇa.*«

[556] *abhijñā.* [557] *laghutva.*

[558] Ch_1: »a mind pure from the outset *(ādiśuddha citta)*«, Ch_2: »to be indifferent and free from covetousness as regards body and life.«

[559] *māyā.* Ch_2: »to cognize all the *dharmas* as being illusional,« Ch_1: »the light mind is by its nature like the *māyā.*«

[560] In Ch_1 the text of this point seems corrupt and is not clear.

[561] *avyabhicārin.* [562] *śamatha.*

[563] *pratisaṃvid.* We have here a somewhat free interpretation of the four normal *pratisaṃvids: artha-pratisaṃvid, dharma-pratisaṃvid, nirukti-pr.* and *pratibhāna-pr.* The fact that in our text *artha* is put as the first *pratisaṃvid* is one proof more that this text belongs to the earlier strata of Mahāyānistic Scriptures, see Har Dayal, *The Bodhisattva Doctrine* p. 264.

[564] *artha.* [565] *vyañjana.* Ch_1: »adornment *(maṇḍana).*«

[566] *dharma.*

[567] *i. e.* the etymology *(nirukti).*

reality[568] and 4. having known that the words[569] are inexhaustible[570], to teach the doctrine being free from every attachment and hindrance[571]. These are the four [comprehensions].

115. The Bodhisattvas, Bhadra, endowed with four *dharmas* attain the following principles which have to be born in mind[572]. What are these four? 1. to be insatiable in striving for the great learning[573], 2. to have veneration and devotion towards those possessed of the great learning[574], 3. to apply oneself always to teach the doctrine to others[575] and 4. to aim at understanding the hidden sense of the Tathāgata's teaching by means of setting words and letters in the right order[576].

116. By the Bodhisattvas, Bhadra, endowed with four *dharmas* the following [kinds] of forbearance[577] are attained. What are these four? 1. faith[578], 2. not to turn back from their way, 3. unanimity[579] and 4. tirelessness[580]. Those are the four [kinds of forbearance].

---

568 *anātma*. In Ch_1 this point seems to be represented by the end of point 2 which means: »unoriginated and not disappearing.« Ch_2: »to know that all the *dharmas* are beyond the *nirukti*.«

569 *akṣara*.

570 *akṣaya*. Ch_1 translates only this part as the 3rd point. It confounds *akṣara* with *akṣaya* as it means: »to know that all which is *akṣaya* is *akṣaya*.« Ch_2: »relying upon the *akṣaras*, to teach inexhaustibly.«

571 *asakta* and *apratihata*, two usual epithets of the *pratibhāna*. In Ch_1 this second part of the sentence constitutes the 4th point.

572 *dhāraṇī*. The context points out clearly that it is not the usual meaning of *dhāraṇī*: »magical spell« which is concerned here.

573 *bahuśrutatva*. 574 Ch_1 links both first points into one.

575 In Ch_1 it constitutes the 2nd point, Ch_2 om. it.

576 Ch_1: »by means of understanding all the words of the teaching without making mistakes about the sense«, Ch_2: »by means of teaching the true meaning of various words.« Both Ch. divide this sentence into two points.

577 *kṣānti*. 578 *adhimukti*.

579 T. *tshogs* = *sāmagrya*. Ch_2: »assembling of wealth *(bhogasampad)*« which does not suit the series of *kṣāntis*.

580 The items enumerated in Ch_1 are quite different: »(1) [the Bodhisattvas] lead to salvation *(tārayanti)* those who are not yet saved, (2) they lead to deliverance those who are not yet delivered, (3) they all have pleasure in the *dharma* *(dharmarata)* and (4) they do not annihilate good conduct.«

117. By the Bodhisattvas, Bhadra, endowed with four *dharmas* the following abilities in discussion[581] are attained. What are these four? 1. not to contradict when somebody else expounds the doctrine, 2. to have reverence for the teacher of the doctrine and to listen respectfully to his teaching, 3. not to boast of one's own learning and 4. not to treat contemptuously those who have little learning. These are the four [abilities].

118. The following are, Bhadra, the four [kinds] of turning away[582] of the Bodhisattvas. What are these four? 1. the turning away from passion, hatred and infatuation, 2. the turning away from the *śrāvakas*[583], 3. the turning away from the *pratyekabuddhas* and 4. the turning away of the discriminative consciousness[584] from the evil *dharma*[585]. These are the four [kinds of turning away].

119. Four *dharmas*, Bhadra, constitute for the Bodhisattvas the insight into the profound sense. What are these four? 1. to cognize the conditioned *dharmas*[586] as dependently originated[587], 2. to cognize the hidden sense [of the teaching][588], 3. to cognize one's own nature[589] and 4. to conceive all the *dharmas* in one sense, *i. e.* cognizing them as being void[590]. These are, Bhadra, the four insights....

120. The following, Bhadra, are the vows to be fulfilled by the Bodhisattvas endowed with four *dharmas*. What are these four? 1. perfectly pure virtue[591] and training[592], 2. purification

---

[581] *pratibhāna.*

[582] T. *bsgyur-ba* = *vivarttana* (?). The translation of Ch_1 *pu t'ui chuan* by the negation *pu* probably renders the prefix *vi-*, but this is not a very successful translation because it corresponds usually to *avivarttana*, a notion of exactly opposite meaning.

[583] Ch_1: »beings«. [584] *saṃjñā.*

[585] *akuśaladharma.* This reading is preserved only in Ch_1. Ch_2 = *kuśaladharmalakṣaṇa* and T. = *kuśalamūladharma.* Ch_1 interchanges the 3rd and 4th points.

[586] *saṃskṛtā dharmāḥ,* so Ch_2. T. and Ch_1 om.

[587] *pratītyasamutpanna.* Ch_1 translates the entire point as follows: »to cognize the 12 *nidānas*«.

[588] *saṃdhi,* cf. foot-note 493. Ch_1 om. this point.

[589] Ch_1 adds: »and to cognize rightly the *buddhamārga*«, Ch_2: »to cognize rightly the proper nature of all the *dharmas.*«

[590] Ch_1 adds, as the 4 point: »to cognize the *buddhadharma.*«

[591] *śīla.* [592] *śikṣā.* Ch_1 = *kṣānti*, Ch_2 om.

from obscuration caused by deeds[593], 3. absence of treachery[594] and 4. energy in striving for the attainment of the store of merits[595]. These are, Bhadra, the vows to be fulfilled....

121. The Bodhisattvas, Bhadra, who are endowed with four *dharmas* and who have reached all the perfections[596] possess the following qualities enabling them not to turn back[597]. What are these four? 1. he who is endowed with skilfulness[598] can accumulate on one perfection[596] all the remaining perfections, 2. he who is endowed with skilfulness, if he knows the nature of one being, can conceive [the nature] of all other beings[599], 3. he who is endowed with skilfulness, if he realizes one kind of perfectly pure[600] *dharmas*, may realize all the other perfectly pure *dharmas* and 4. if he has reached the Absolute, he may believe in all the Buddhas through one Buddha[601]. The Bodhisattvas, Bhadra, who are endowed with these four *dharmas* and who reached all the perfections, possess these qualities which enable them not to turn back.

122. When the Lord had expounded these 4 achievements, he juggler Bhadra attained the acceptance of the doctrine that all the *dharmas* are without origination[602] and was pleased, delighted, enraptured, rejoiced and very satisfied and, as a result of this great joy, he rose up to the skies to the height of seven palm-trees[603].

At that very moment the Lord smiled and, as a a result of that smile, there issued from his mouth innumerable and immeasurable rays of light which pervaded all the Buddha-lands[604] and turned back to the *uṣṇīṣa* of the Lord. Then the venerable

---

593 *karmāvaraṇa*. 594 *śaṭhya*.

595 Ch_2: »to increase the *kuśalamūla*.«

596 *pāramitā*. 597 *avaivarttikā dharmāḥ*.

598 *upāyakauśalya*, Ch_1 om.

599 Ch_1 adds: »...as being inexistent.«

600 Ch_1: »free from passion.«

601 Ch_1: »through the *dharmakāya* of one Buddha«, Ch_2 adds: »And why? Because the essence of all the *dharmas* is undifferentiated (*nirviśeṣa*).«

602 *anutpattikadharmakṣānti*.

603 Ch_1: »to the height of 49 feet.«

604 *buddhakṣetra*. Ch_2 = *lokadhātu*, Ch_1 om. the entire passage concerning the rays of light.

Ánanda rose from his seat and, after throwing his robe over one shoulder, fixed his right knee on the ground and, lifting up his clasped hands before the Lord, addressed him in these words[605]: »Sir, the Lord Tathāgata does not smile without cause or reason. What is the cause and what is the reason of Thy smiling?«

And he uttered the following stanzas:

123. »O source of knowledge, famous by Thy immeasurable splendour[606] and wisdom, famous in all the three worlds as the one who attained the perfection of merits[607], o Victorious One who is selfsprung[608], ruler of mankind[609], please explain me what for hast Thou smiled?

124. O Thou who knowest the mental attitudes[610] of all the beings, as many as there are of them in all the spheres[611] of the Universe, Thou who knowest the lowest, the most exalted and also the intermediary [attitudes][612] — please explain me the purpose of Thy smiling.

125. The voices of the gods sitting here, of *kinnaras*, men, Śakra, *asuras*, *garuḍas*[613], *mahoragas*, Brahma and all the other voices[614], can they, if only in part[615], equal[616] the immaculate voice of the Buddha?

126. The shine of the effulgent sun, the brightness of jewels and the splendour of Śakra and Brahma are pervaded

---

[605] Ch$_2$ »thought in his mind«, Ch$_1$ om.

[606] *tejas*. Ch$_1$ adds: »which surpasses the [splendour] of the sun and of the moon.«

[607] *guṇapāramitā*. Ch$_2$: »who attained the *bodhi* and the *guṇapāramitā*.«

[608] *svayaṃbhu*, Ch$_2$ om. [609] Both Ch. om.

[610] *cittacaryā*. [611] *gati*, Ch$_2$: »5 *gatis*.«

[612] Ch$_1$ adds: »[the attitudes] of the eminent men who are free from attachments.«

[613] Ch$_1$ = *gandharvas*.

[614] Ch$_2$: »the various voices uttered by men, gods and the great eightfold assembly.«

[615] Ch$_2$: »smallest part *(kalā)*.« Perhaps T. *ga-la*, the syntactical value of which is not very clear, is a misreading for *ka-la* = skr. *kalā* ?

[616] I have corrected *spyod* (attested in all T. recensions) into *phod* in accordance with Ch. Cf. a similar confusion *phod*/*spyod* in § 35. Both Ch.: »they cannot equal.«

by the light of Buddha [and in comparison with this brightness they look as if] they did not shine at all[617].

127. O Thou who art Buddha, who hast attained the profound *dharma*, who hast understood that beings are void, without personality[618] and without individuality[619], who has rejected[620] both extremities: that of existence and that of non-existence, who knows that transient reality[621] is [illusory as is the reflection] of the moon in water, —

128. do now tell those whose mind is inclined towards the best Vehicle[622], who belong to the lineage[623] of Buddha and to the lineage of *dharma*, who contribute to the growth of the Three Jewels[624], — tell them why Thou hast smiled?

129. When the Victorious One teaches the doctrine to the *śrāvakas,* [the rays issuing from] the smile of the Sugata come back to his knees; if he addresses the Vehicle of the *pratyekabuddhas*[625], [the rays] return to his shoulders. But when he speaks to the [adherents of] the Buddha's Vehicle, [the rays] return to the top of his head.

---

[617] Ch_2: »The effulgence of the moon, the sun and the jewels, the shining of Śakra and all the brightness of Brahma are darkened, cease to be and shine no more when Buddha emits light which illuminates all the Buddhalands *(buddhakṣetra).*« Ch_2: »The effulgence of the Lord pervades the entire Universe and illuminates the immeasurable Buddhalands. The brightness of the sun, the moon and of jewels cannot equal that of the Tathāgata.«

[618] *anātma.* [619] *apudgala.* Ch_1 = *ajīva.*

[620] In Ch_1 the reading *chüan* of the »Three editions« and the »Old Sung ed.« should be substitued to *sun* of Taishō.

[621] literally: »the three Times« *i. e,* the empirical reality which passes through the past, the present and the future. Ch_1: »who knows that wordly happiness is illusional like moonlight.«

[622] Ch_1: »Path.«

[623] *gotra.* Ch_1 om. and translates: »who are grounded in the *buddhamārga* and the *saddharma.*«

[624] *triratna.*

[625] T. *rkyen-gyi theg-pa*, a rather unusual rendering of *pratyekabuddhayāna.*

130. As hundreds of thousands of rays emitted by Thee came back to the *uṣṇīṣa* of the Sugata, there are no doubts that Thou, the god of gods[626] and the benefactor of beings dost now the benefit of prophesying to some one the attainment of the Buddha's Vehicle[627].«

131. Thereupon the Lord thus spoke to the venerable Ānanda: — »Hast Thou seen, Ānanda, the noble youth[628] Bhadra?[629]« — »Yes, Lord, I have seen him«, — he replied. — »Then, Ānanda, this noble youth Bhadra, after 92 000[630] aeons, during an aeon called »Well Created[631]«, in a world called »the Great Arrangement[632]« will appear as the Tathāgata, the Arhat, the Fully Enlightened One[633] — Vikurvaṇarāja[634] by name. And

[626] *devātideva.*

[627] Both Ch. differ considerably in the rendering of the matter of stanzas 129, 130. Ch_1: »(129) when the Buddha teaches the pure doctrine to the *śrāvakas*, the rays which lean on him (?) shine like the light of all the suns. Things are different when he expounds the highest Truth to those wishing to become Buddhas. (130) In order to have no doubts, I ask Thee, god of gods, to explain me who will attain the *buddhayāna*. This effulgence of the Buddha, pure and removing defilements has come back to Buddha, to the top of his head and is seen no more.«

Ch_2: »(129) The rays which are emitted by the smile of the Tathāgata behave in different ways according to the Vehicle. They come back to his knees or his shoulders if [Buddha addresses] the men of two Vehicles (*dviyāna*). (130) But the immeasurable rays which he emitted now reach the *uṣṇīṣa* of the Tathāgata. Then, for whom is meant the prophecy of the god of gods concerning the attainment of the *buddhayāna*?« Leumann's translation of these two stanzas (see L. p. 365) is based on Ch_2.

[628] *kulaputra*. In T. Bhadra is thus called only from this § onward, cf. foot-note 383. In Ch_1 »the juggler« is still used, but *kulaputra* appears already in the next sentence.

[629] Ch_1 adds: »... [Bhadra] lifted up to the skies.«

[630] So all the versions. Leumann (L. p. 365) prefers »92 aeons« without any foundation.

[631] *Sunirmita* T. *legs-par-sprul-pa* = Ch_1 *huan hua* = Ch_2 *shan hua.*

[632] *Mahāvyūha.* T. *bkod-pa-chen-po* = Ch_2 *ta chuang yen.* Ch_1 *ta ching* consists in a misreading *Mahāśuddha.*

[633] Ch_1 gives the full list of epithets, as *e. g.* in § 3.

[634] T. *rnam-par-'phrul-ba'i rgyal-po* = Ch_1 *yen ching wang* = Ch_2 *shen pien wang.* Leumann (L. p. 365, note 2) points out that a Buddha called Sarvaguṇeśvaraprabhāsa-vikurvaṇarāja is mentioned in the *Śūraṃgamasamādhi.* In the *lokadhātu* of this Buddha as well, only the Bodhisattvas and no *śrāvakas* or *pratyekabuddhas* are found.

the »Great Arrangement« world belonging to this Tathāgata Arhat, Fully Enlightened One Vikurvaṇarāja will be very rich, extensive and delightful, very abundant[635], pleasant and full of men and numerous beings. It will be flat like the palm of the hand, soft to the touch like the *kācalindi*[636] stuff, adorned with flowery trees[637], resounding with various musical sounds. Multifarious incenses will burn there and, continually, without interruption, umbrellas, banners and flags will be hoisted.

As for food and drink, Ānanda, just as the enjoyments of the Thirty Three[638] are obtained at the mere thought of them, so will be obtained the enjoyments and the feeding of the inhabitants [of this world]. And in the »Great Arrangement« world various arrangements will appear constantly, therefore this world will be called »the Great Arrangement«.

All the beings of this Buddha-land will possess a great faith and will exclusively profess the religion of the Great Vehicle. The Tathāgata Vikurvaṇarāja will live 10 000 years, and even after his *parinirvāṇa* his holy religion will last still ten million years[639]. And, Ānanda, at the very moment of the extinction of the Tathāgata Vikurvaṇarāja he will prophesy to the Bodhisattva Viśrutakīrti[640] (?) that [in future times this Bodhisattva] will appear on earth as the Tathāgata, the Arhat, the Fully Enlightened One — Samantaspharaṇapati[641] by name. After this prediction Vikurvaṇarāja will meet complete extinction.

132. Thereupon the noble youth Bhadra descended from the skies, bent his head to the feet of the Lord and thus spoke: — »O Lord, from this day onward I take refuge in all the million millions of Buddhas, Tathāgatas, Arhats and Fully Enlightened Ones, in the Holy Teaching and in the Holy Congregation! And

---

635 *subhikṣa*. 636 Ch_2: »*tulapaṭika* stuff.«

637 Ch_1: »trees shining with the brightness of the sun and of the moon«, Ch_2: »flowers, fruits, trees and creepers *(vallī)*.«

638 Ch_1 adds: »in the palace of seven treasuries.«

639 Ch_1: »100 000 years.«

640 T. *sgra-rnam-par-grags-pa* = Ch_1 *wen ch'eng* = Ch_2 *ch'eng*$_1$. Leumann (ibid.) proposes the reconstruction: *Yaśas.*

641 T. *kun-gyi-khyab-bdag* = Ch_1 *p'u ta* = Ch_2 *i chieh tsui sheng.* Leumann proposes *Sampūrṇapati.*

I shall proclaim the Absolute Essence[642] of the Tathāgata in the same way as it was explained by the Tathāgata himself by means of his own Absolute Essence which does not differ from the Absolute[643], which is indivisible[644], without imperfection[645], undifferentiated[646], unborn[647] and unconditioned[648]«.

133. Then the venerable Ānanda addressed the noble youth Bhadra in these words: —, »O Bhadra, hast thou reached the Absolute Nature[649] of the Tathāgata? For thou speakest just like Tathāgata speaks about the Absolute Essence[650].« Bhadra replied: — »All the *dharmas*, Ānanda, reached the Absolute Nature of the Tathāgata. Why? Because, Ānanda, the Tathāgata has recognized the Absolute Essence as being indivisible. I have cognized also this Absolute Essence as being indivisible, and just as I have cognized it, so have all the beings. And just as it concerns all the beings, so it concerns all the *dharmas*. Therefore, o venerable Ānanda, duality is not the true aspect[651] of the Absolute Nature of the Tathāgata.

The non-duality, o venerable Ānanda, can neither be perceived, nor cognized by anybody[652]. Why? Because the knowledge

---

642 *tathatā*.

643 properly speaking: »is not wrong *(aviparita)* [in relation to the real *tathatā]*.«

644 *abhedya*. 645 ***avikala***. 646 *akalpita*. 647 *anutpanna*.

648 *anabhisaṃskṛta*. Ch. translate this passage as follows: Ch_1 »Just as the Tathāgata is inexistent from the outset ***(pen wu)***, so all the Buddhas do not differ from him as they are also inexistent from the outset; this *tathatā* is *abhedya*, *acala*, *akalpita*, *anutpanna*, *anabhisaṃskṛta* and *advaya*. The Tathāgata is inexistent from the outset and therefore I shall accomplish a similar *tathatā*.«

Ch_2: »I shall take refuge in the *tathatā* just as does the Lord Buddha who shows by means of his own *tathatā* which is not different from the [real] *tathatā*, that all the *dharmas* do not differ from the *tathatā*, that they are *nirviśeṣa*, *avikala*, *akalpita*, *anutpanna* and *anabhisaṃskṛta*. Leumann's translation of this passage is not exact.

649 *dharmatā*.

650 *tathatā*. Ch_1 continually renders it as »non existence from the outset *(pen wu)*.«

651 = *na dvayaprabhāvita*. For the translation of *prabhāvita* see R. p. 65 foot-note 152.

652 Ch_1: »only those who use discriminative imagination *(saṃjñā)* conceive plurality.«

of one who knows [that the world is but] imaginated[653] is the knowledge of Buddha.«

Thereupon the venerable Ānanda said to the Lord: — »O Lord, this noble youth Bhadra can turn the head of all the world including gods. Formerly he turned heads by means of the essence of illusion and now he does it by means of his wisdom and knowledge[654]. And for what reason? Because such is the power of his wisdom and knowledge[655].«

134. Then the Lord spoke thus to the juggler Bhadra: — »Bhadra, art thou able to deceive all the world including gods?[656]« He replied: — »Just as the Lord deceives, so I deceive. And why? Because *e. g.* the Lord, though there exists no »self«[657], teaches the Truth using the conventional word »beings«, and, though there exist no soul[658] and no individual person[659], the Lord, when teaching the Truth, adopts the word »person«. Therefore he is a great deceiver. After having reached the Highest Essence of Enlightenment[660] he does not see any *dharma* which dies, transmigrates or is born, and yet he teaches the doctrine of death, transmigration and rebirth[661]. As such is the Lord, he appears in whatever place of the world of men and gods as if he were a Tathāgata proclaiming the Truth[662].«

The Lord approved the juggler Bhadra with the words: —

[653] literally: »who knows the *saṃjñā*.« Ch_1: »to reject the *saṃjñā* means to reach the knowledge of the Buddha.« Ch_2: »to cognize all the *dharmas* as being but imagined (= as being but *saṃjñā*) is the knowledge of the Buddha.«

[654] Ch_2 adds: »... and the *pratibhāna*.«

[655] Ch_1 translates this passage as follows: »Ānanda said to the Lord: — »Should the noble youth Bhadra now preserve his magical power by means of which he deceived gods and men?« Buddha answered to Ānanda: — »Now Bhadra attained the *māyā* of the *dharmajñāna*. Why? Because it is the *pratibhāna* of his wisdom.«

[656] Ch_2 briefly: »is it true, Bhadra?«

[657] *ātman*. [658] *jīva*. [659] *pudgala*. [660] *bodhimaṇḍa*.

[661] Ch_1: »the Tathāgata is inexpressible *(anakṣara)* and did not attain the *bodhimaṇḍa*. Can then the *dharmas* which die, are born or transmigrate exist? And yet [The Buddha] teaches the doctrine of death and rebirth.«

[662] Ch_1: »there exists no *nirvāṇa* and yet he shows the *nirvāṇa*. Since the Lord teaches that all is equal, he can deceive all the world including gods because he shows that all the merits *(guṇa)* are equal.« Ch_2 om. this all and repeats only: »The Tathāgata is the great deceiver.«

»Well said, well said, noble youth! It is really as Thou tellst, *viz.*: though there exists no »self«, I teach the Truth using the conventional word »beings«, and, though there exist no soul and no individual person, when teaching the Truth, I adopt the word »person« and this is a great deceit. Furthermore, the Tathāgata, after having reached the Highest Essence of Enlightenment, does not see any *dharma* which dies, transmigrates or is born, and yet he teaches the doctrine of death, transmigration and rebirth. [In the absolute aspect] there exists no *nirvāṇa* nor any doctrine which is taught in order to make the *nirvāṇa* possible[663].«

135. Then the noble youth Bhadra expressed to the Lord the wish of being ordained and the Lord said to the Bodhisattva Maitreya: — »Do ordain[664], Maitreya, the noble youth Bhadra.« Maitreya ordained and consecrated Bhadra and addressed thereafter the Lord in these words: — »O Lord, the ordination of a Bodhisattva does not consist in these [ritual] appearances[665], marks and formalities[666]. Why, o Lord? Because no Bodhisattva is attached to all these external marks. The [true] ordination of the Bodhisattvas is to remain in the three worlds in order to bring beings to maturity[667].«

Thereupon, in consequence of this instruction, the mind of 5000 beings became directed to the Supreme Enlightenment and the mind of 200 monks[668] became free from attachments[669] and delivered from defilements[670].

136. Then the venerable Ānanda asked the Lord: — »How should be called, o Lord, this exposition of the doctrine?[671] Which name should we bear in our minds?« The Lord answered: — »Bear in your minds[672] [the name] »The Prophecy

---

663 Ch_1 om., Ch_2: »Though there exist no *dharma* which can be called *nirvāṇa*, I teach the *nirvāṇa* in order to make salvation possible.«

664 Both Ch.: »shave his hair and beard and make him a *śramaṇa*.«

665 literally: »colours *(varṇa)*«. Ch_2 translates *erh* »ear«, an obvious misreading: *karṇa* instead of *varṇa*.

666 T. *tshul* = *ākāra* »proceedings.« $Ch_{1, 2}$: *hsing*$_2$ »forms.«

667 Ch_1: »in order to attain perfect wisdom.«

668 Ch. om. 669 *anupātta*. Both Ch. om.

670 *āsravavinirmukta*. 671 *dharmaparyaya*.

672 T. *zuṅ(s)-śig* = *dhārayitavyam* and not *dhāraṇī* as Leumann translates it (L. p. 366).

concerning the juggler Bhadra[673]« or »The Gradual Attaining of Enlightenment« [674].«

A Bodhisattva[675], Ānanda, who wishes to behold the Tathāgata and who wishes to do the work of Buddha for the sake of beings, must keep this exposition of the doctrine, bear it in mind, read it and explain it to others. What for? Because, Ānanda, he who kept it, bore it in mind, read it and explained it to others can behold the Tathāgata and can do the work of Buddha for beings. Therefore, Ānanda, for the sake of the bliss of numerous beings, owing to affection for the world, in order to bring profit, advantage and happiness to gods and men, keep this exposition of the doctrine, bear it in the mind, read it and master it. The *dharmas*, Ānanda, which will attain Enlightenment, attain it through the Great Vehicle and they learn it by the Great Vehicle. Therefore this exposition of the doctrine may also be called: »The Attaining of Enlightenment«.

Thou shouldst believe in it, Ānanda, and fix it in thy mind. And in him who will put this exposition of the doctrine in a book and who will nourish it in his self, the Tathāgata will abide in his body and how much more in the body of those who, having heard it, shall realize the Absolute Essence[676].«

137. Thereupon the noble youth Bhadra thus spoke to the Lord: — »This exposition of the doctrine, o Lord, should also be called: »The incitement of the store of former merits«. Why? Because, o Lord, after my having heard this exposition of the doctrine, the formerly accumulated store of my merits became manifest.«

Thus taught the Lord. And the noble youth Bhadra, the venerable Ānanda, the whole host of assistants, and the world including gods, men, *asuras* and *gandharvas* applauded in ecstasy to the words of the Lord.

---

[673] *Bhadra-māyākāra-vyākaraṇa.*

[674] *Samyaksaṃbodhikrameṇotpatti.*

[675] Ch_2: »a being who, in the future, wishes to behold the Buddha.«

[676] *tathatā.* Ch_2: »...shall rightly undersand this book (?).« Ch_1 is not clear.

Bhadra-māyākāra-vyākaraṇa

według źródeł tybetańskich i chińskich.

Streszczenie polskie

Ārya-Bhadra-Māyākāra-vyākaraṇa należy do bardzo ważnej, a mało jeszcze dotąd zbadanej grupy sutr mahajanistycznych, zwanej *Ratnakūṭa*. Oryginał sanskrycki tekstu nie został zachowany. Mamy jedynie przekłady: tybetański (Kandżur, *Dkon-brtsegs-pa* 21, tłumacze: Jinamitra, Prajñāvarma, Ye-śes-sde) oraz dwa przekłady chińskie: starszy z III/IV wieku po Chr. (tłumacz Dharmarakṣa) i późniejszy z epoki dynastii T'ang (tłumacz Bodhiruci, który działał pomiędzy 693 a 713 rokiem). Wobec tego, że przekład Dharmarakṣy nie bardzo się różni od przekładów późniejszych, możemy z dużym prawdopodobieństwem przypuścić, że tekst oryginalny miał już mniej więcej obecną postać w II/III wieku, należy więc do okresu powstawania najstarszych sutr mahajanistycznych.

Treścią sutry jest legenda o czarowniku imieniem Bhadra, który przy pomocy sztuczek magicznych chciał oszukać Buddę, zapraszając go na ucztę magiczną, wyczarowaną na śmietniku. Budda nie tylko przejrzał podstęp, ale przy pomocy swej potęgi magicznej sprawił, że Bhadra, nie mogąc cofnąć swych czarów, uznaje wyższość Buddy nad sobą i nawraca się. Legendę tę spotykamy na terenie buddyjskim w dwu innych redakcjach późniejszych od redakcji sanskryckiej, ale chyba od niej niezależnych. Prawdziwie literackie opracowanie opowiadania znajdujemy w wersji »sakijskiej«, zachowanej w cyklu tekstów buddyjskich, wydanych przez Ernesta Leumanna (*Das nordarische sakische Lehrgedicht des Buddhismus*, Leipzig 1933, str. 6—26). Reminiscencję legendy spotykamy również w tradycji palijskiej (Komentarz do *Dhammapady*, wydanie Normana, I 435—45), gdzie jednak ostał się tylko zasadniczy motyw uczty, nie ma natomiast ani postaci czarownika, ani też z tą legendą nie są związane żadne wnioski doktrynalne. Jedynie w wersji sanskryckiej, leżącej u podstawy znanych nam tekstów tybetańskich i chińskich, legenda o czarowniku jest kanwą, na której rozsnute są ogólne rozważania doktrynalne, przede wszystkim nauka o tym, że wszystko jest māyą, kosmiczną iluzją. Podstęp Bhadry służy tu za punkt wyjścia dla wykładu tej nauki. Ponieważ Bhadra wie, że wyczarowana przez niego uczta na prawdę nie istnieje, nie jest mu trudno zrozumieć, że podobnie iluzoryczną jest cała rzeczywistość empiryczna. Analogia pomiędzy małym czarownikiem Bhadrą a Buddą — czarownikiem uniwersalnym, jest szczegółowo rozwinięta. Różnica pomiędzy obu czarownikami jest ilościowa i jakościowa: *māyā* Bhadry jest częściowa, jednostronna (*ekadeśa*), podczas gdy *māyā* Buddy dotyczy całej rzeczywistości. Poza tym, »oszukańcze« stworzenie przez Buddę iluzorycznej rzeczywistości ma cele dobre, prowadzi istoty do zbawienia. Bhadra natomiast wyczarował swoją ucztę w złych zamiarach. Jednakże wobec tego, że wszelka ofiara złożona Buddzie, nawet w złych celach, liczy się jako zasługa, oszukańcza uczta Bhadry ma pewną pozytywną wartość, zwłaszcza że dała okazję do nawrócenia samego Bhadry i obecnych przy uczcie. Właściwą jednak ofiarą w tym wypadku jest zrozumienie nierealności świata fenomenalnego.

Imię Bhadry nie jest przypadkowe. W tradycji buddyjskiej nazywają się tak przeważnie siewcy niezgody, schizm i herezyj. Tradycja południowa zachowała pamięć o mnichu, zwanym Subhadda, który po śmierci Buddy próbował wzniecić bunt w gminie buddyjskiej. W tradycji północnej spotykamy postać pewnego Bhadry, który został mnichem w 137 roku po Nirwanie i zajmował się wyszukiwaniem punktów spornych w piśmie, wywołując w ten sposób zwątpienie i niesnaski. Dopiero po jego śmierci poznano, iż był on wcieleniem Māry. Mamy tu prawdopodobnie reminescencję boga zniszczenia, Śiwy, którego jednym z imion było właśnie Bhadra.

Cały tekst odznacza się rzadką w literaturze buddyjską jednolitością treści, którą przerywają jedynie §§ 79—121 zawierające wyliczenia cech i obowiązków Bodhisatwów w typowej dla sutr buddyjskich klasyfikacji czwórkowej.

Praca niniejsza zawiera krytyczną edycję tekstu tybetańskiego oraz t. zw. krytyczne tłumaczenie czyli przekład oparty na wszystkich wersjach tybetańskich i chińskich i uwzględniający w odnośnikach wszystkie odchylenia od przyjętej interpretacji. Wobec tego, że szczegółowy tybetańsko-chiński indeks ma się ukazać osobno, do pracy niniejszej dodany jest jedynie indeks zrekonstruowanych terminów sanskryckich oraz spis chińskich słów cytowanych w książce.

TRANSLATION OF POLISH SUMMARY

The *Ārya-Bhadra-Māyākāra-vyākaraṇa* belongs to a very important yet still unsufficiently investigated group of Mahāyāna sūtras, called *Ratnakūṭa*. Its Sanskrit original is not preserved; we possess only one Tibetan translation by Jinamitra. Prajñāvarman, Ye śes sde (Kanjur, *dkon brtsegs pa* 21), and two Chinese translations: by Dharmarakṣa from the 3rd/4th century A.D. and by Bodhiruci from the period of T'ang dynasty (Bodhiruci was active 693-713 A.D.). Since Dharmarakṣa's translation does not differ too much from the later translations it can be surmised with much probability that the original text has acquired more or less the present form in the 2nd or 3rd centuries A.D. Thus it belongs to the period of origination of the oldest Mahāyāna sūtras.

The contents of the Sūtra is a legend of a juggler Bhadra. Bhadra, due to his magical tricks, intended to deceive the Buddha and invited him to a magic feast which was charmed into being on a refuse dump. The Buddha, however, not only saw through the stratagem but also through his magical power made Bhadra, who could not revoke his charms, to acknowledge Buddha's superiority and converted him.

In the Buddhist literature the legend is found in two other versions, later than the Sanskrit version but probably independent from it. A genuine literary version one can find in Khotanese: it is preserved in a series of Buddhist texts edited by Ernst Leumann (*Das nordarische sakische Lehrgedicht des Buddhismus*, Leipzig 1933, pp. 6-26). There is a reminiscence of the legend in the Pali tradition, viz. in the commentary on the Dhammapada (ed. Norman, I, pp. 435-445). Here, however, only the principal motive of a feast has been preserved, while the person of a juggler as well as all the doctrinal consequences of the legend are absent. It is only the Sanskrit version that was the basis of the above mentioned Tibetan and Chinese texts, where the general doctrinal speculations and in particular the doctrine of the *māyā*, i.e. that everything is but a cosmic illusion, are focused on the person of the juggler. Bhadra's trick is a starting point for the teaching. Since Bhadra knows that the feast created by him does not exist in reality it is not difficult for him to understand a similar illusionary nature of the empirical reality. This analogy between Bhadra the juggler and the Buddha, a universal magician is developed in details. There is a quantitative and qualitative difference between the two magicians: Bhadra's *māyā* is partial only, one-sided (*ekadeśa*), while the Buddha's *māyā* refers to the whole reality. Moreover, Buddha's "false" creation of the illusory reality has good ends—it leads the sentient beings to liberation; Bhadra created his feast with an evil intention. However, every gift offered to the Buddha, be it done even with a bad intention, is regarded as a merit, and therefore Bhadra's deceitful feast has nonetheless some positive value. The more so as it brought to Bhadra's conversion and all those taking part in the feast. But as the true gift is here regarded realization of nonreality of the phenomenal world.

The name of Bhadra does not seem to be accidental—in the Buddhist tradition it is often given to dissidents, heretics and schismatics. According to the Southern tradition, a monk, Subhadda by name, tried to organize a dissent in the sangha after Buddha's death. According to the Northern tradition, a certain Bhadra, who became a monk 137 years after the Nirvāṇa, was tracing controversial points in the Scriptures and provoked doubts and quarrels within the sangha; only after his death he has been recognized as an incarnation of Māra, the Evil One. Most probably this is a reflection of Śiva, god of destruction, one of his name being just Bhadra.

The text itself is very homogeneous in its contents, a rare feature in the Buddhist literature; only paragraphs 79-121 contain a list of the characteristics and the duties of a bodhisattva in a typical Buddhist tetradic classification.

The present work contains a critical edition of the Tibetan text and a so-called critical translation, i.e. an annotated translation based on all the Tibetan and Chinese versions. In the foot-notes are recorded all the deviations from the accepted interpretation.

Warsaw, January 1990 DR. MAREK MEJOR

INDEX

Sanskrit — Tibetan

As a detailed Tibetan, Chinese and Sanskrit Index will appear in a separate volume, the present list contains only those technical terms and proper names, the Sanskrit reconstruction of which is given in the foot-notes of the »critical translation«. When the word is missing in the Tibetan version or is reconstructed only on the basis of Chinese versions, it is given in the Index without the T. equivalents.

Numbers without specification refer to the foot-notes, those preceded by § or p. refer to the numbers of paragraphs and pages respectively.

Proper names

Technical terms and expressions

List of the Chinese Words occurring in the Text

(see the Table which follows)

1. an wen.
2. ch'ang che.
3. ch'ang lai.
4. ch'ang ying.
5. ch'ao.
6. ch'eng.
7. ch'eng$_1$.
8. chi hsiang.
9. chi i.
10. ch'i.
11. chiao shai.
12. chiang fu (ch'i hsin).
13. chien ku.
14. chien t'a ho.
15. chih$_1$.
16. chih$_2$.
17. chih pao shu.
18. chih tsu.
19. ch'ih huo.
20. ch'ing ching.
21. ch'ing ching shih nü.
22. chu chih.
23. ch'u.
24. chui chu.
25. chung shang.
26. chü.
27. chüan.
28. ch'üan.
29. erh.
30. erh$_1$.
31. fan chih.
32. fan yin sheng.
33. fang pien.
34. fo yen.
35. fu.
36. hen.
37. ho$_1$.
38. ho$_2$.
39. hou.
40. huan hua.
41. hui yen.
42. hsiang.
43. hsiang ch'u.
44. hsieh hsing chih shu.
45. hsieh i tao.
46. hsin.
47. hsin chü.
48. hsing$_1$.
49. hsing$_2$.
50. hsien.
51. hsü.
52. i.
53. i chieh tsui sheng.
54. i tao.
55. jen hsien.
56. jen ming.
57. ju.
58. k'ai hua (jen).
59. kan lu.
60. kou na.
61. k'u chieh.
62. kuan.
63. kuang ching.
64. kuang ming.
65. kuei.
66. kung.
67. ling.
68. ming.
69. ming chio.
70. nien.
71. pen wu.
72. p'i lan p'o.
73. p'ing teng hsing.
74. p'ing teng p'u chien.
75. po li chih to chü pi t'o lo.
76. po li t'u na.
77. po t'o lo.
78. p'o t'o.
79. pu k'o te.
80. pu t'ui chuan.
81. p'u ta.
82. p'u t'i hsin.
83. san.
84. se hsiang.
85. so p'o shih chieh chu.
86. su$_1$.
87. su$_2$.
88. sui lan.
89. sun.
90. ssŭ ch'i hsing.
91. shan hua.
92. shan nan tzŭ.
93. shen.
94. shen li.
95. shen pien wang.
96. sheng.
97. sheng chieh.
98. ta ching.
99. ta chuang yen.
100. tao.
101. tao hsin.

102. tao i.
103. tao yüan.
104. teng ming.
105. t'i huan yin.
106. t'ien.
107. tuan chieh.
108. ts'ui p'o p'eng.
109. tsun.
110. tsun chung.
111. ts'ung.
112. wai tao.
113. wang fen pieh.
114. wei.
115. wei an chu.
116. wei chi hsi.
117. wei ch'ing liang.
118. wei kan chieh.
119. wei ku tung.
120. wei meng yen.
121. wei p'iao san.
122. wei pien chu.
123. wei sui huai.
124. wen.
125. wen ch'eng.
126. wu.
127. wu ai.
128. wu chi.
129. wu ch'u.
130. wu hsiang hsi.
131. wu hsing chih shu.
132. wu i.
133. wu so li.
134. yen ching wang.
135. yin.
136. yin$_1$.
137. yin$_2$.
138. yin kai.
139. yü ch'ih.

1 安 穩
2 長 者
3 常 來
4 常 應
5 超
6 乘
7 稱
8 髻 相
9 寂 意
10 起
11 澆 灑
12 降 伏 其 心
13 堅 固
14 犍 沓 和
15 知
16 志
17 殖 寶 樹
18 止 足
19 熾 火
20 清 淨
21 清 淨 士 女
22 住 止
23 處
24 追 逐
25 衆 上
26 句
27 捐
28 勸
29 二
30 耳
31 梵 志
32 梵 音 聲
33 方 便
34 佛 眼
35 夫
36 恨
37 合
38 和
39 後
40 幻 化
41 慧 眼
42 向
43 想 處
44 邪 行 之 術
45 邪 異 道
46 信
47 心 句
48 行

49 形
50 限
51 虛
52 亦
53 一 切 最 勝
54 異 道
55 仁 賢
56 人 明
57 如
58 開 化 人
59 甘 露
60 拘 掷
61 枯 竭
62 觀
63 光 淨
64 光 明
65 歸
66 功
67 令
68 命
69 明 覺
70 念
71 本 無
72 毘 嵐 婆

73 平等行
74 平等普見
75 波利質多俱鞞陀羅
76 波栗屠那
77 跋陀羅
78 颰陀
79 不 可 得
80 不 退 轉
81 普 達
82 菩 提 心
83 三
84 色 相
85 娑 婆 世 界 主
86 蘇
87 酥
88 隨 嵐
89 損
90 四 器 行
91 善 化
92 善 男 子
93 神
94 神 力
95 神 變 王
96 生

97 勝解
98 大淨
99 大莊嚴
100 道
101 道心
102 道意
103 道願
104 燈明
105 提桓因
106 天
107 斷截
108 摧破崩
109 尊
110 尊重
111 從
112 外道
113 妄分別
114 爲
115 爲安住
116 爲止息
117 爲清涼
118 爲乾竭
119 爲鼓動
120 爲猛焰
121 爲飄散
122 爲遍霔
123 爲碎壞
124 穩
125 聞稱
126 無
127 無礙
128 無極
129 無處
130 無想悉
131 無形之樹
132 無異
133 無所立
134 嚴淨王
135 隱
136 陰
137 蔭
138 陰蓋
139 愚癡

Tabulated List of corresponding Paragraphs of the Tibetan Text and the Two Chinese Versions in Taishō

(31 a, 6_4 = page 31, first column from above, line 6, character 4 from above)

§ of T.	Ch_1 (Taishō XII, 324)	Ch_2 (Taishō XI, 310_{21})	§ of T.	Ch_1	Ch_2
1	31a, 6_1	486b, 15_1—486b, 26_2	31	32c, 21_1	488b, 4_1
2	31a, 13_{ult}	486c, 8_{10}—486c, 10_{16}	32	32c, 26_1	488b, 7_1
3	31a, 15_{11}	486b, 26_3—486c, 8_9	33	33a, 13_5	488b, 22_{11}—488b, 28_4
4	31a, 24_3	486c, 10_{17}	34	33a, 21_1	488c, 2_1—488c, 3_{10}
5	31b, 4_9	486c, 14_{11}	35	33a, 23_9	488b, 29_1 - 488c, 1_{10}
6	31b, 9_5	486c, 18_{10}	36	33a, 26_5	488c, 4_1
7	31b, 14_{16}	486c, 26_4	37	33a, 29_1	488c, 6_1
8	31b, 20_{15}	487a, 3_1	38	33b, 2_9	488c, 6_1
9	31c, 2_1	487a, 12_3	39	33b, 5_5	488c, 12_1
10	31c, 19_{11}	487b, 5_1	40	33b, 8_1	488c, 14_1
11	31c, 24_3	487b, 10_1	41	33b, 10_9	488c, 16_1
12	32a, 4_{10}	487b, 16_3	42	33b, 13_5	488c, 19_1
13	32a, 10_{10}	487b, 22_6	43	33b, 16_1	488c, 21_1
14	32a, 18_4	487b, 27_4	44	33b, 18_9	488c, 23_1
15	32a, 25_{12}	487c, 1_{17}	45	33b, 21_5	488c, 25_1
16	32a, 29_{12}	487c, 8_1	46	33b, 24_1	488c, 27_1
17	32b, 9_7	487c, 15_2	47	33b, 26_9	488c, 29_1
18	32b, 13_{16}—32b, 20_2	487c, 18_3	48	33b, 29_5	489a, 2_1
19	om.	487c, 26_7	49	33c, 3_1	489a, 4_1
20	32b, 21_1	487c, 29_1	50	33c, 5_9	489a, 6_1
21	32b, 24_1	488a, 3_1	51	33c, 8_5	489a, 8_1
22	32b, 27_1	488a, 6_1	52	33c, 11_1	489a, 12_1
23	32c, 1_1	488a, 9_1	53	33c, 13_9	489a, 13_1
24	32c, 4_1	488a, 12_1	54	33c, 17_1	489a, 15_1
25	32c, 7_1	488a, 15_1	55	33c, 20_9	489a, 19_1
26	32c, 10_1—32c, 12_{10}	488a, 18_1	56	33c, 23_5	489a, 21_1
27	om.	488a, 22_1	57	33c, 26_1	489a, 24_1
28	32c, 13_1	488a, 25_1	58	33c, 28_9	489a, 27_1
29	32c, 15_1	488a, 27_1	59	34a, 2_5	489a, 29_1
30	32c, 18_1	488b, 1_1	60	34a, 5_1	489b, 3_1

§ of T.	Ch_1	Ch_2	§ of T.	Ch_1	Ch_2
61	34a, 7_9	489b, 5_1	100	35b, 1_7	490c, 2_{10}
62	34a, 10_5	489b, 8_1	101	35b, 3_{13}	490c, 4_{14}
63	34a, 13_{10}	489b, 10_1	102	35b, 6_6	490c, 8_3
64	34a, 15_9	489b, 12_1	103	35b, 9_3	490c, 11_8
65	34a, 18_5	489b, 14_1	104	35b, 14_{10}	490c, 17_{12}
66	34a, 21_1	489b, 16_1	105	35b, 17_7	490c, 20_{17}
67	34a, 23_9	489b, 19_1	106	35b, 20_8	490c, 21_1
68	34a, 26_5—34a, 28_{12}	489b, 22_1	107	35b, 22_{13}	490c, 23_4
69	om.	489b, 25_1	108	35b, 25_7	490c, 27_6
70	34b, 2_9—34b, 5_4	489b. 27_1	109	35b, 28_{12}—35c, 2_9	491a, 3_7
71	33a, 29_1 -34b, 2_8	489c, 1_1	110	35c, 8_{15}—35b, 13_8	491a, 5_{10}
72	34b, 5_5	489c, 4_1	111	35c, 2_{10}	491a, 10_{15}
73	34b, 8_1	489c, 7_1	112	35c, 5_1—35c, 8_{14}	491a, 14_3
74	34b, 10_9	489c, 9_1	113	35c, 13_9	491a, 19_3
75	34b, 14_1	489c, 12_1	114	35c, 16_7	491a, 22_5
76	34b, 18_1	489c, 16_1	115	35c, 19_{16}	491a, 25_6
77	34b, 20_1	489c, 18_1	116	35c, 23_1	491a, 28_7
78	34b, 22_{17}	489c, 21_{13}	117	35c, 25_4	491b, 1_{10}
79	34b, 29_8	489c, 28_3	118	35c, 28_3	491b, 4_{11}
80	34c, 3_9	490a, 3_3	119	36a, 2_4	491b, 7_{13}
81	34c, 5_{12}	490a, 5_{11}	120	36a, 4_{16}	491b, 10_{14}
82	34c, 8_{10}	490a, 9_5	121	36a, 7_8	491b, 12_{17}
83	34c, 11_7	490a, 11_{15}	122	36a, 12_7	491b, 20_1
84	34c, 13_{10}	490a, 14_1	123	36a, 16_1	491b, 27_1
85	34c, 15_{13}	490a, 16_1	124	36a, 20_1	491b, 29_1
86	34c, 19_1	490a, 19_3	125	36a, 24_1	491c, 2_1
87	34c, 22_3	490a, 22_4	126	36a, 28_1	491c, 4_1
88	34c, 25_6	490a, 25_5	127	36b, 3_1	491c, 6_1
89	34c, 29_3	490a, 28_6	128	36b. 7_1	491c, 8_1
90	35a, 2_9	490b, 1_{12}	129	36b, 11_1	491c, 10_1
91	35a, 5_6	490b, 4_{17}	130	36b, 15_1	491c, 12_1
92	35a, 8_7	490b, 8_1	131	36b, 19_1	491c, 14_1
93	35a, 11_1	490b, 11_6	132	36c, 6_2	491c, 27_1
94	35a, 13_5	490b, 14_3	133	36c, 12_1	492a, 3_{17}
95	35a, 16_2	490b, 16_{10}	134	36c, 23_1	492a, 13_9
96	35a, 18_{14}	490b, 19_{11}	135	37a, 2_{14}	492a, 22_{10}
97	35a, 23_4	490b, 23_{16}	136	37a, 10_1	492b, 1_{16}
98	35a, 25_{16}	490b, 26_6	137	37a, 19_6—37a, 24_4	492b, 13_3—492b, 17_8
99	35a, 28_4	490b, 29_7			

Corrigenda

Page	line	instead of	read
6	10 from below	oversion	version
8	15	§ 100	§ 110
52	16 from below	*sṅon-kyi*	*sṅon-gyi*
58	18 from below	Ch_1 *po t'o*	Ch_1 *p'o t'o*
58	4 from below	*māyāvidya°*	*māyāvidyā°*
63	3 from below	word	world
67	4 from below	*ping t'o lo*	*pi t'o l'o*